DATE DUE

AUG 0 2 2012	

Psychological
Disorders

Tourette Syndrome

Psychological Disorders

Psychological
Disorders

Tourette Syndrome

M. Foster Olive, Ph.D.

Series Editor
Christine Collins, Ph.D.
Research Assistant Professor of Psychology
Vanderbilt University

Foreword by
Pat Levitt, Ph.D.
Director, Vanderbilt Kennedy Center
for Research on Human Development

CHELSEA HOUSE
P U B L I S H E R S
An imprint of Infobase Publishing

Tourette Syndrome

Chelsea House
An imprint of Infobase Publishing
132 West 31st Street
New York NY 10001

Library of Congress Cataloging-in-Publication Data
Olive, M. Foster.
  Tourette syndrome / M. Foster Olive ; consulting editor, Christine Collins ;
foreword by Pat Levitt.
     p. cm. — (Psychological disorders)
  Includes bibliographical references and index.
  ISBN-13: 978-1-60413-426-1 (hardcover : alk. paper)
  ISBN-10: 1-60413-426-7 (hardcover : alk. paper) 1. Tourette syndrome.
I. Collins, Christine E. (Christine Elaine) II. Title. III. Series.
  RC375.O45 2010
  616.8'3—dc22   2009024427

Text design by Keith Trego
Cover design by Keith Trego and Alicia Post

Printed in the United States of America

Bang EJB 10 9 8 7 6 5 4 3 2 1

This book is printed on acid-free paper.

Table of Contents

Foreword

Pat Levitt, Ph.D.
Vanderbilt Kennedy
Center for Research
on Human Development

Think of the most complicated aspect of our universe, and then multiply that by infinity! Even the most enthusiastic of mathematicians and physicists acknowledge that the brain is by far the most challenging entity to understand. By design, the human brain is made up of billions of cells called neurons, which use chemical neurotransmitters to communicate with each other through connections called synapses. Each brain cell has about 2,000 synapses. Connections between neurons are not formed in a random fashion, but rather are organized into a type of architecture that is far more complex than any of today's supercomputers. And, not only is the brain's connective architecture more complex than any computer; its connections are capable of *changing* to improve the way a circuit functions. For example, the way we learn new information involves changes in circuits that actually improve performance. Yet some change can also result in a disruption of connections, like changes that occur in disorders such as drug addiction, depression, schizophrenia, and epilepsy, or even changes that can increase a person's risk of suicide.

Genes and the environment are powerful forces in building the brain during development and ensuring normal brain functioning, but they can also be the root causes of psychological and neurological disorders when things go awry. The way in which brain architecture is built before birth and in childhood will determine how well the brain functions when we are adults, and even how susceptible we are to such diseases as depression, anxiety, or attention disorders, which can severely disturb brain function. In a sense, then, understanding how the brain is built can lead us to a clearer picture of the ways in which our brain works, how we can improve its functioning, and what we can do to repair it when diseases strike.

Brain architecture reflects the highly specialized jobs that are performed by human beings, such as seeing, hearing, feeling, smelling, and moving. Different brain areas are specialized to control specific functions. Each specialized area must communicate well with other areas for the brain to accomplish even more complex tasks, like controlling body physiology—our patterns of sleep, for example, or even our eating habits, both of which can become disrupted if brain development or function is disturbed in some way. The brain controls our feelings, fears, and emotions; our ability to learn and store new information; and how well we recall old information. The brain does all this, and more, by building, during development, the circuits that control these functions, much like a hard-wired computer. Even small abnormalities that occur during early brain development through gene mutations, viral infection, or fetal exposure to alcohol can increase the risk of developing a wide range of psychological disorders later in life.

Those who study the relationship between brain architecture and function, and the diseases that affect this bond, are neuroscientists. Those who study and treat the disorders that are caused by changes in brain architecture and chemistry are psychiatrists and psychologists. Over the last 50 years, we have learned quite a lot about how brain architecture and chemistry work and how genetics contributes to brain structure and function. Genes are very important in controlling the initial phases of building the brain. In fact, almost every gene in the human genome is needed to build the brain. This process of brain development actually starts prior to birth, with almost all the neurons we will ever have in our brain produced by mid-gestation. The assembly of the architecture, in the form of intricate circuits, begins by this time, and by birth we have the basic organization laid out. But the work is not yet complete because billions of connections form over a remarkably long period of time, extending through puberty. The brain of a child is being built and modified on a daily basis, even during sleep.

While there are thousands of chemical building blocks, such as proteins, lipids, and carbohydrates, that are used much like bricks and mortar to put the architecture together, the highly detailed connectivity that emerges during childhood depends greatly upon experiences and our environment. In building a house, we use specific blueprints to assemble the basic structures, like a foundation, walls, floors, and ceilings. The brain is assembled similarly. Plumbing and electricity, like the basic circuitry of the brain, are put in place early in the building process. But for all of this early work, there is another very important phase of development, which is termed experience-dependent development. During the first three years of life, our brains actually form far more connections than we will ever need, almost 40 percent more! Why would this occur? Well, in fact, the early circuits form in this way so that we can use experience to mold our brain architecture to best suit the functions that we are likely to need for the rest of our lives

Experience is not just important for the circuits that control our senses. A young child who experiences toxic stress, like physical abuse, will have his or her brain architecture changed in regions that will result in poorer control of emotions and feelings as an adult. Experience is powerful. When we repeatedly practice on the piano or shoot a basketball hundreds of times daily, we are using experience to model our brain connections to function at their finest. Some will achieve better results than others, perhaps because the initial phases of circuit-building provided a better base, just like the architecture of houses may differ in terms of their functionality. We are working to understand the brain structure and function that result from the powerful combination of genes building the initial architecture and a child's experience adding the all-important detailed touches. We also know that, like an old home, the architecture can break down. The aging process can be particularly hard on the ability of brain circuits to function at their best because positive change comes less readily as we get older. Synapses may be lost and brain chemistry can change over time. The difficulties in understanding how architecture gets built are paralleled by the complexities of what happens to that architecture as we grow older. Dementia associated with brain deterioration as a complication of Alzheimer's disease and memory loss associated with aging or alcoholism are active avenues of research in the neuroscience community.

There is truth, both for development and in aging, in the old adage "use it or lose it." Neuroscientists are pursuing the idea that brain architecture and chemistry can be modified well beyond childhood. If we understand the mechanisms that make it easy for a young, healthy brain to learn or repair itself following an accident, perhaps we can use those same tools to optimize the functioning of aging brains. We already know many ways in which we can improve the functioning of the aging or injured brain. For example, for an individual who has suffered a stroke that has caused structural damage to brain architecture, physical exercise can be quite powerful in helping to reorganize circuits so that they function better, even in an elderly individual. And you know that when you exercise and sleep regularly, you just feel better. Your brain chemistry and architecture are functioning at their best. Another example of ways we can improve nervous system function are the drugs that are used to treat mental illnesses. These drugs are designed to change brain chemistry so that the neurotransmitters used for communication between brain cells can function more normally. These same types of drugs, however, when taken in excess or abused, can actually damage brain chemistry and change brain architecture so that it functions more poorly.

As you read the Psychological Disorders series, the images of altered brain organization and chemistry will come to mind in thinking about complex diseases such as schizophrenia or drug addiction. There is nothing more fascinating and important to understand for the well-being of humans. But also keep in mind that as neuroscientists, we are on a mission to comprehend human nature, the way we perceive the world, how we recognize color, why we smile when thinking about the Thanksgiving turkey, the emotion of experiencing our first kiss, or how we can remember the winner of the 1953 World Series. If you are interested in people, and the world in which we live, you are a neuroscientist, too.

Pat Levitt, Ph.D.
Director, Vanderbilt Kennedy Center
for Research on Human Development
Vanderbilt University
Nashville, Tennessee

Overview of Tourette Syndrome

Kevin was 12 years old when he started having symptoms of Tourette syndrome. For no apparent reason, he began pulling on his ear lobe a few times per day. Eventually, the frequency of his ear pulling increased to approximately every five minutes, but there were times of the day when he didn't pull on his ear at all.

At first Kevin just thought he was nervous about an upcoming oral book report he was to give in class. Kevin found that he could not stop pulling on his ear lobe no matter how hard he tried. He also started grunting occasionally for no apparent reason. When the time came to give his book report, he grunted numerous times and continued to pull at his ear, and some of his fellow students started to point, whisper to each other, and laugh. After the book report, Kevin's teacher asked him if something was bothering him and why he kept tugging on his ear and grunting. He said he was just nervous. But even after the book report was over, the grunting and ear pulling continued. His friends started asking him, "Why do you keep doing that?" But Kevin just shrugged his shoulders, thinking it would go away on its own. But it didn't, and Kevin became increasingly embarrassed by the teasing from his schoolmates.

Since Kevin often grunted and tugged at his ear at home, his parents became very concerned that Kevin might have some sort of psychological problem, and they took him to see a child psychologist. The psychologist said that there was probably underlying anxiety that was making Kevin fidget and pull on his ear and *grunt, but to be safe the psychologist referred Kevin to a neurologist. The neurologist, who had treated hundreds of patients with a variety of neurological disorders over the span of his 30-year career, was immediately convinced that Kevin had Tourette syndrome. The doctor prescribed a medication that would help Kevin reduce his repetitive ear pulling and grunting, and also referred Kevin to a behavioral therapist who could teach Kevin how to voluntarily control these distressing behaviors. The neurologist also gave Kevin's parents some information about Tourette syndrome and the name of a local support group that helped patients with Tourette syndrome and their families cope with the disorder.*

After months of medication and therapy, Kevin was able to get his ear pulling and grunting habits under control to the point where he only did them three to four times a day. The distress that this problem caused Kevin began to fade, as did the teasing and harassing from his fellow students.

Long thought to be a result of psychological problems or even possession by evil spirits, **Tourette syndrome** (also called *TS, Tourette's syndrome, Gilles de la Tourette syndrome,* or *Tourette's disorder)* is a neurological condition caused by malfunctioning of the brain, and most scientific evidence suggests that this disorder has a genetic origin. The primary symptom of Tourette syndrome is the repeated display of **tics**. **Motor tics** are repeated involuntary movements of parts of the body, particularly the head, neck, face, or legs. **Vocal tics** (or **phonic tics**) are repeated involuntary noises, ranging from simple grunts and coughs to complex phrases and sentences. People with Tourette syndrome display both motor tics and vocal tics. Examples of various types of tics will be discussed in more detail in Chapter 2.

In order to be diagnosed with Tourette syndrome, a person must meet the following criteria: (1) the presence of vocal and motor tics, although they need not occur at the same time;

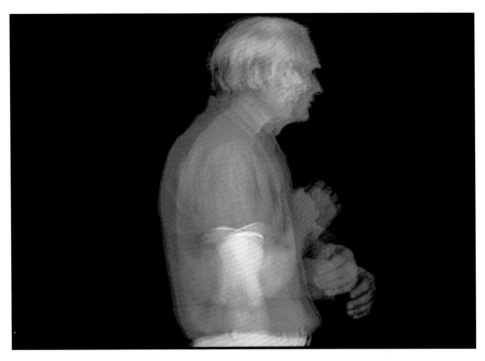

Figure 1.1 Repetitive movements of the head and neck are a common type of tic in Tourette syndrome. *(Time & Life Pictures/Getty Images)*

(2) the tics must be exhibited frequently (i.e., multiple times per day) for more than a year, and the person cannot go without displaying some type of tic for more than three months; (3) the motor tic must shift between different body parts over time, and the number, frequency, and type of tic must also change over time; (4) the symptoms must become present before the age of 18; and (5) the tics cannot be explained by another medical condition or a side effect of a medication.[1]

Oftentimes in people with Tourette syndrome, a "premonition" type of feeling comes on right before the tic, as if the person can feel the tic about to occur. Once the tic is performed, this feeling goes away, and most often performing the tic is the only way to make this premonitory feeling subside. People with

TS can sometimes voluntarily suppress a tic if they feel one coming on, but are only able to do so for a short period of time before the tic is eventually involuntarily carried out.

The most common age at which people develop symptoms of Tourette syndrome is during childhood. It has been estimated that as many as 10 percent of all children develop some form of tic at least once during childhood, but most often these tics disappear with age. Less than 2 percent of all children actually go on to develop a diagnosable form of TS.[2] Tics tend to worsen as the child grows into late childhood and adolescence. Symptoms tend to lessen when the patient reaches adulthood, but for most TS patients the tics never disappear completely. TS is equally common across all ethnicities and racial backgrounds, but is three to four times more prevalent in boys than girls. More of the demographic characteristics of TS will be discussed in Chapter 3.

Although Tourette syndrome has been around for centuries, one of the first cases of this disorder described in the medical literature was the Marquise de Dampierre, a woman who lived in France from 1799 to 1884.[3] This upper-class, intelligent, well-mannered woman was known for blurting out obscenities in the middle of otherwise normal conversations. The marquise was often surprised and embarrassed by her own vocal tics, as were the people around her when these vocal tics occurred. Physician Jean-Marc Gaspard Itard reported this unusual case in a medical journal, and noted that this lady was so embarrassed by her own involuntary obscenities that she became extremely afraid of uttering them, and the process of worrying about the tics brought them into her conscious mind, ultimately rendering her unable to control them.[4]

Approximately 60 years following the publication of Itard's case report of the Marquise de Dampierre, a French neurologist named Georges Gilles de la Tourette gathered together

Figure 1.2 Jean-Marc Gaspard Itard, one of the first physicians to medically document the symptoms of Tourette syndrome. *(National Library of Medicine)*

eight additional cases of people with this type of motor or vocal tic and called this syndrome a "maladie (illness) of tics" in an article he published in 1885.[5] Gilles de la Tourette's mentor, a doctor named Jean-Martin Charcot, decided to name the illness Gilles de la Tourette Syndrome, which is now more commonly referred to as Tourette or Tourette's syndrome.

As mentioned earlier, there is substantial scientific evidence that Tourette syndrome is a biological malfunction of the brain. This malfunction is largely genetic in nature, since it has been shown that if one identical twin (who shares the exact same DNA of his or her sibling) develops TS, there is a greater than 50 percent chance that his or her twin will also develop TS. Neurological studies in patients with TS have shown that they have abnormal regulation of the chemical messenger **dopamine** in the brain. This will be discussed in further detail in Chapter 4.

Tourette syndrome typically is treated with a combination of psychological and behavioral therapies and medications. Since TS is a result of a biological malfunction of the brain, psychological and behavioral therapies alone are less successful in treating TS than using them in combination with medications. Medications that affect the activity of the brain's chemical messenger dopamine appear to be the most beneficial in reducing the symptoms of TS. Over the last several decades, neurosurgical techniques have also been developed that are effective in treating severe forms of Tourette syndrome. Despite the success of medical treatments, which are discussed in detail in Chapters 5 and 8, these treatments must be accompanied by psychological or behavioral therapies in order to obtain the highest level of containment of TS symptoms. For example, education of family members, friends, and the TS patient about the disorder helps those involved become better able to cope with it. Identifying potential triggers of tics also helps in the management of the symptoms. Stress management techniques, such as exercise and relaxation therapies, can be used to help reduce the incidences of tics and the anxieties they provoke. Other behavioral therapies, such as habit reversal training, can also be useful in reducing the severity of Tourette syndrome, and these will be discussed in Chapter 6.

As one might imagine, the sudden blurting out of an obscenity or repeatedly performing a seemingly bizarre behavior such as ear pulling, especially when in a public place, can cause an extreme amount of stress and embarrassment for the TS patient and his or her friends and family. Since Tourette syndrome develops during childhood, often the afflicted child is subjected to a significant amount of teasing, bullying, or isolation by

Psychiatric Disorders Commonly Associated with Tourette Syndrome

Although the bizarreness of the tics associated with Tourette Syndrome might make one think it is a rare and isolated disorder, there are several other psychiatric disorders that are commonly observed in patients with Tourette Syndrome. One of these is obsessive-compulsive disorder (OCD), which is an anxiety disorder characterized by repeated, intrusive, unwanted thoughts or fears (called *obsessions*) that often result in the person performing some type of motor act (called a *compulsion*) in an attempt to relieve the discomfort caused by the obsession. One of the most common types of obsession is the thought of being contaminated by germs, which causes the person to wash his or her hands repeatedly throughout the day to a point where it interferes with his or her social life, education, or occupation. Another disorder commonly seen in people suffering from Tourette Syndrome is attention-deficit/hyperactivity disorder (ADHD), in which the person has a hard time concentrating and is hyperactive, impulsive, and disruptive to others. People with Tourette Syndrome often exhibit signs of OCD or ADHD, and likewise, people with OCD or ADHD may often have some form of tic that might indicate they also have Tourette Syndrome.

classmates. Therefore, the TS patient as well as his or her friends and family need to develop coping strategies for dealing with tics. The inability of the child to control his or her tics, as well as the social consequences of them, often results in a great deal of anger in the child, and anger management strategies must be employed. These coping strategies are discussed in detail in Chapter 8.

• • • • • • • •

SUMMARY

Tourette syndrome is characterized by repeated motor and vocal tics that develop during childhood. There is evidence that Tourette syndrome is a genetically inherited malfunction of the brain. People with Tourette syndrome, as well as their families, often suffer a substantial degree of embarrassment, stigmatism, stress, and anger, and need to be taught how to cope with the disorder. Tourette syndrome often is associated with symptoms of other psychiatric disorders such as OCD and ADHD. Tourette syndrome is treated with psychological and behavioral therapies as well as medications. In more severe cases, surgery on the brain is needed to control the severity of the tics.

Symptoms of Tourette Syndrome

Perhaps one of the most famous people in history believed to have Tourette syndrome (TS) was the classical music composer Wolfgang Amadeus Mozart (1756–1791).[1] Mozart was a childhood musical genius, having written his first symphony by the age of eight. Evidence that he might have suffered from TS comes from letters to his cousins and other family members, which frequently contained vulgar language pertaining to the anus and defecation. He even wrote an obscenely titled music piece referring to the human hind parts. Mozart also showed some evidence of motor tics, including bizarre facial expressions and repetitive movements of the hands and feet. In addition, Mozart's family noted that he was very hyperactive, suggesting he might have had ADHD as well. Furthermore, he had a tremendous irrational fear of leaving his wife at home alone, and was extremely meticulous about personal hygiene, suggesting that he might have had symptoms of OCD. Although it is impossible to comprehensively "diagnose" a person who is no longer living (and thus cannot be observed by mental health professionals to determine if the patient meets the current specific diagnostic criteria for a certain mental or neurological disorder), many historians and physicians believe that Mozart's repeated use of vulgarity and repetitive body movements indicate that he had TS.

In order for a person to be diagnosed with Tourette syndrome, he or she must meet the following criteria as set forth by the current (fourth) edition of the *Diagnostic and Statistical Manual of Mental Disorders* (DSM-IV):[2]

- both multiple motor tics and one or more vocal tics must be present at the same time, although not necessarily concurrently;
- the tics must occur many times a day (usually in clusters or "bouts") nearly every day or intermittently over more than one year, during which time there must not have been a tic-free period of more than three consecutive months;
- the age at onset of the symptoms must be less than 18 years; and
- the disturbance must not be due to the direct physiological effects of a substance (e.g., a stimulant such as cocaine) or another medical condition.

Since the main feature of TS is the presence of tics, this is usually what physicians focus on when making a diagnosis. The physician, usually a neurologist, will focus on the anatomical location of the tic (i.e., whether it occurs in the face, hands, feet, etc.), the number of times the tic is repeated (i.e., whether a person flails his or her arm once or five times in a particular episode), the frequency of the tic (i.e., how many times per day the tic occurs), the duration of the tic (i.e., how long it takes to complete it), and the length of time the person has been suffering from the tics. These features of tics are incorporated into various rating scales used by neurologists.[3] Some of these rating scales are simple questionnaires about a patient's history of tic behavior, such as the Tourette Syndrome Symptom List; the Tourette Syndrome Questionnaire; The Motor Tic, Obsessions and Compulsions, Vocal Tic Evaluation Survey; and the Ohio Tourette Survey Questionnaire. Other rating scales combine these questionnaires with actual observances of the tics by the neurologist, including Tourette Syndrome Global Scale, the Yale Global Tic Severity Scale, the Hopkins Motor and Vocal Tic Scale, the Tourette Syndrome Diagnostic Confidence Index, and the Shapiro Tourette Syndrome Severity Scale. Use of these scales allows doctors to make comparisons of the severity of symptoms before and after treatment, across ethnicities and genders, and within families for genetic studies.

It should be noted that both motor and vocal tics are necessary for the patient to meet the criteria for a diagnosis of Tourette syndrome. If only motor tics are apparent, the disorder is called **chronic motor tic disorder** (CMTD), and if only vocal tics are present, the disorder is called **chronic vocal tic disorder** (CVTD).[4] In addition, tics must be present for several years. If a tic only lasts between four weeks and 12 months, the disorder is called **transient tic disorder** (TTD).

MOTOR TICS

Motor tics are repetitive movements of parts of the body. Motor tics can be classified as simple tics or complex tics.[5] Simple tics are very sudden, brief (usually less than 1 second in duration), and repetitive movements such as eye blinking, turning the head to one side, making unusual facial expressions (sometimes called "grimacing"), shrugging of the shoulders, jerking movements of the arms or legs, and tapping or stomping of the feet. Often patients with Tourette syndrome that are very young (i.e., less than four years old) and are completely unaware of the tic. However, over time most people with TS go on to develop more complex tics, which are sudden, repetitive movements that are of longer duration. Examples of complex motor tics include brushing back the hair, deep knee bends, bending the torso, stepping backward, or doing a 360-degree spin on one foot. Motor tics can also be vulgar, consisting of obscene hand

Figure 2.1 A TS patient displaying a facial expression motor tic, often called a grimace. *(ARCD/Rudolf/age fotostock)*

or finger gestures or lewd protrusions of the tongue. In rare cases, tics can involve harming of the self (see sidebar). Patients with TS are usually aware of their more complex tics, and the embarrassing social impact they have on themselves and others. Motor tics are typically the first symptom of TS to emerge, usually appearing around the age of seven; age of onset can range, however, from two years to 18 years.[6]

VOCAL TICS
The other type of tic symptomatic of Tourette syndrome is a vocal tic, sometimes called a phonic tic. These are sudden, repeated, and purposeless sounds that are made by the

When Tics Go Bad: Malignant Tourette Syndrome

In Tourette syndrome, motor tics are usually harmless flinching of the muscles in the face, neck, arms, or legs, and can be simple or complex in nature. However, in approximately 5 percent of patients with TS, motor tics can actually result in harm to the patient, which is called self-injurious behavior. When self-injurious behavior occurs in a patient with TS, the disorder is called malignant Tourette syndrome.[7] Examples of tics displayed by these patients include:

- repeated pounding of a fist on the abdomen resulting in bruising and internal organ damage

- hitting oneself in the eye

- intentional gagging of oneself by placing foreign objects in the throat

- stabbing oneself in the neck with a knife

- repeated biting of the lip until it bleeds and needs stitches

- repeated stomping of the foot until hip dislocation occurrs

- burning of the forearm with a cigarette lighter

- violent head and neck jerks that result in whiplash or other neck or spine injuries

Self-injurious behaviors like these are commonly observed in patients with other psychiatric disorders, such as severe depression, autism, and OCD. However, when it occurs in conjunction with tics, it is considered malignant Tourette syndrome. Most often these patients require hospitalization and antidepressant or antipsychotic medications, but successful elimination of these behaviors is difficult to obtain.[8]

patient. Like motor tics, vocal tics can be simple or complex in nature. Examples of simple vocal tics are repeated clearing of the throat, grunting, barking, coughing, whistling, or making high-pitched squeaks. Examples of more complex tics are repeated imitations of sounds or words spoken by others (called **echolalia**), repetition of sounds or words spoken by the TS patient (called **palilalia**, which often resembles stuttering), repeated utterances of nonsensical words or phrases, and repeated blurting out of obscenities, curse words, or racial slurs (called **coprolalia**). Some vocal tics are mumbled unrecognizably, while others are spoken at a normal tone of voice or even shouted out. Recalling the story of the Marquise de Dampierre in Chapter 1, this upper-class, well-mannered French woman would often unwillingly shout the phrase, "Filthy *[obscenity]* pigs!" at people as they passed by, or at friends and family members.[9] Her utterances of this obscene phrase were extremely distressing to her, as they were involuntary and incongruent with her normal personality and manner. Not surprisingly, this vocal tic caused great embarrassment and stigma to the woman and her family. Profane vocal tics can, at times, lead to personal injury, since a nearby person may be so offended by the TS patient's vocal tic that he or she might be physically assaulted. However, coprolalia occurs in only a minority (approximately 8 to 10 percent) of TS patients.[10]

Vocal tics can occur independently of motor tics, or can be emitted before, during, or after a motor tic, forming an orchestrated sequence. For example, a patient might turn his or her head to one side and then back again, followed by a snorting sound. In assessing the intensity and severity of vocal tics, physicians will assess the frequency and duration of the tic as well as the volume at which it is emitted and the degree to which it disrupts normal speech and nearby activities. Motor and vocal tics can occur once every few moments to once every few hours. Tics can even occur while the patient is sleeping or can cause the patient to have trouble falling asleep.

During childhood, when the symptoms of Tourette syndrome first appear, tics almost always start off as motor tics, and as the child ages, vocal tics emerge, and the two together become increasing complex in nature.[11] However, the tic may increase or decrease its frequency over time (called "waxing and waning"), becoming more intense at certain times in the patient's life (especially during stressful periods), while at other times becoming less problematic.[12] Tics also tend to change in nature over time. For example, for a few months a person may have a tic of rolling his or her eyes repeatedly, which may then evolve into facial grimacing for another few months, then sudden head jerks, and then back to eye rolling. The same is true for vocal tics, where the words or type of sound emitted change over time.

PREMONITIONS OF TICS

Many patients with Tourette syndrome, especially those in adolescence, often have a premonition that a tic is about to occur. They feel as if the urge to perform the tic is building up pressure inside them, and this pressure can only be relieved by executing the tic. They may also feel "itching" or "aching" in a certain part of the body that precedes the tic. For example, a patient may report that his or her throat "itches" immediately prior to a vocal tic, and if he or she doesn't relieve that feeling by vocalizing the tic, the itching continues to build to an unbearable level. In medical terms, these are called **premonitory urges**. When tics are reduced by the natural waning of symptoms or various treatments, the premonitory urges also are reduced. However, these urges are not present for all types of tics, and some tics occur without any warning.

ARE TICS COMPLETELY INVOLUNTARY?

The vast majority of patients with Tourette syndrome would probably answer "yes" to this question, as they feel as if they have very little control over their tics. However, there is evidence that tics are "suggestible," meaning that they can be brought on by talking about them. For example, when a neurologist is attempting to make a diagnosis of a patient with symptoms of TS, he or she might ask the patient about their history of the kinds of tics they have experienced in the past. The mere act of recalling a type of tic that the patient had a number of years ago, and has not had since, might bring about a recurrence of performing that tic.[13] In other words, the revival of a memory of a previous tic might make it occur again, suggesting that the patient may have some control over which type of tic occurs. In addition, with strong focused attention and other mental and behavioral strategies, some TS patients are able to suppress their tics for very short periods of time. However, after this voluntary suppression of a tic, a "rebound" phenomenon tends to occur when the tic is eventually executed, such that its intensity is greater than if that patient had not tried to voluntary suppress it. So, while there is some evidence that tics can be controlled (to a very limited degree) voluntarily, most tics are largely beyond the control of the TS patient.

• • • • • • • •

SUMMARY

The primary symptom of Tourette syndrome is the presence of motor tics (sudden, short, repeated movements of the eyes, tongue, lips, face, head, neck, arms, or legs) and vocal tics (repeated uttering of sounds, words, phrases, or even obscenities). In rare instances, motor tics can be violent and a danger to the TS patient or family members. Tics are often preceded by premonitory urges that give the patient uncomfortable feelings in certain body parts that can only be relieved by executing a tic. Tics are also suggestible and can be voluntarily suppressed, but only for very short periods of time.

Tics begin to appear in childhood and get progressively worse through adolescence. While most TS patients never experience a full disappearance of their tics in adulthood, the severity of tics appears to decrease with age.

3 Prevalence of Tourette Syndrome

Haji was the youngest of five Kenyan children. Haji had an older brother, Kafil, and three older sisters. When Kafil was five years old, he started to display sudden erratic movements of his eyes and lips. By the time Kafil was eight, he also started repeatedly flinching his arms and making a snorting sound.

Not too long after Haji's fourth birthday, he began to develop similar tics of the face, which later evolved into more elaborate motor and vocal tics. None of his three sisters developed any type of tic. Kafil and Haji were often mocked by their classmates at school as well as by children in their neighborhood. The boys often were bullied and occasionally beat up by several older neighborhood children. Because Haji and his family lived in a small poor village, they had no knowledge about Tourette syndrome (TS) as a medical condition. One day after a beating incident, Haji's mother decided to pull the boys out of their school and teach them at home. After several years of having two children with these seemingly bizarre tics, Haji's mother took her two boys to the only village doctor, but he was bewildered by the symptoms that Haji and Kafil exhibited and dismissed them as "nervous habits."

Eventually Haji's mother saved enough money to travel to Nairobi, the capital of Kenya, and stay with some relatives for several weeks. While she was there, she took the boys to see several doctors, one of whom finally referred them to a neurological clinic at the main hospital in Nairobi. There, Haji and Kafil were *diagnosed with TS. However, the only remedies that the clinic could offer were expensive medications, which the family could not afford. Distraught and discouraged, Haji's mother and her family returned to their village without any hope for a cure for the affliction that ostracized them from their friends, family, and school.*

This is a sad but often true story for families with children suffering from Tourette syndrome, especially those who do not have the knowledge or financial means to properly treat the disorder. Although TS is a neurological condition that is mostly genetic and biological in origin, its prevalence, or **epidemiology**, appears to be relatively even across different countries throughout the world. However, there can be some variability in the prevalence of TS among different national and international statistics, which can be a result of a number of factors, including a doctor's appropriate training in recognizing the symptoms of TS, differences in the methods of symptom assessment (i.e., use of a particular rating scale), and access to and affordability of health care, which is typically much lower in underdeveloped countries. This chapter will examine what is known to date about the prevalence of TS worldwide and differences across gender, ethnicities, and socioeconomic status.

WORLDWIDE PREVALENCE

One of the earliest studies conducted on the rate at which Tourette syndrome occurs in the general population was a survey in 1973, which showed that only 430 cases of TS had been reported worldwide in a population of approximately 3.9 billion people, suggesting that the disorder is relatively rare (i.e., one in approximately every nine million people, or 0.0000001 percent).[1] However, this 1973 study was published long before standard medical criteria had been established to properly diagnose TS. By 1984, additional prevalence studies had changed the estimate to 0.05 percent, or one in every

Figure 3.1 Boys are four times more likely to have Tourette syndrome than girls. *(Audrey Aumyagoy/Shutterstock)*

2,000 people, indicating an increase in knowledge and correct diagnosis of TS.[2] As of 2008, estimates place the prevalence of TS at approximately one to two cases in every 100 people.[3] Thus, over the years, the increasing knowledge about TS as a neurological disorder, more widespread use of TS rating scales, and the development of international computerized databases on TS have shown that this disorder, once thought to be very rare, occurs in approximately 1 to 2 percent of the population worldwide.

Some tics that appear during childhood will disappear completely over time on their own, which is called transient tic disorder. This disorder appears to be much more common than that of TS, occurring in 6 to 20 percent of all children.[4] Thus, only a small percentage of children who develop tics actually go on to develop all the symptoms of TS. The prevalence of chronic motor tic disorder and chronic vocal tic disorder is approximately equal to that of TS (i.e., 1 to 2 percent).[5]

GENDER DIFFERENCES

Tourette syndrome occurs more frequently in males than females by a ratio of approximately four to one. Why are male children more prone to develop TS than female children? Thus

Table 3.1

COUNTRY	PERCENTAGE OF TS PATIENTS WHO ARE MALE
China	82%
Ecuador	72%
Greece	88%
Korea	81%
Pakistan	90%
South Africa	75%
Sweden	74%

Tourette syndrome is consistently more prevalent in male versus female children worldwide. As seen in this data collected by Dr. Mary Robertson of University College of London, the percentage of TS patients who are male in various countries across the world generally lies between 75 and 90 percent, which is equivalent to a male-to-female ratio of approximately four to one.

Source: M.M. Robertson, "The prevalence and epidemiology of Gilles de la Tourette syndrome. Part 1: the epidemiological and prevalence studies," *Journal of Psychosomatic Research* 65 (2008): 461–72.

far, scientists have not been able to find evidence of a gene or genes located on the male sex chromosome that might be linked to TS. It has been speculated that the presence of male hormones such as testosterone during fetal development may influence the

Pockets of Isolation: Geographical Areas Where the Incidence of Tourette syndrome Is Lower than Normal

The prevalence of Tourette Syndrome (TS) is generally the same across all cultures and ethnicities.[7] However, there have been a few reports that in certain geographic areas the prevalence of TS is lower than worldwide estimates. For example, in the greater metropolitan area of the city of Wenzhou in the People's Republic of China, a survey of medical records of 9,742 people found that only 42 were identified as having TS, yielding a prevalence of 0.43 percent, less than half of that which is estimated worldwide.[8] Even more intriguing, in a province of South Africa dominated by people speaking the Xhosa language (sometimes called the Xhosa Province), a total of 1,506 cases of TS were documented out of a population of 327,473 medical patients, yielding a prevalence of 0.05 percent, approximately 20 times lower than that of the worldwide prevalence.[9] Why are the rates of TS in these particular geographic regions lower than normal? Researchers are still not quite sure, but possible reasons include: (1) the fact that in some regions life-threatening medical conditions such as AIDS or malaria take precedence over TS,w or (2) in many countries, particularly those with vast rural and underdeveloped areas, doctors and the public are not well educated about TS. The possibility also exists that since TS is largely a genetic disorder, there may be certain populations of humans that do not carry the defective gene or genes that may cause TS, or may carry a gene that protects against developing TS.[10]

development of the brain and predispose the child to become more likely to develop TS.[6] As a result of exposure of the fetal brain to testosterone, male brains may be fundamentally different from female brains, even down to the level of DNA, and these differences may make males more prone to develop TS. However, these are currently theories with only limited scientific support, and more research is needed to find out why there is such a higher prevalence of TS in male children.

SOCIOECONOMIC STATUS

Because Tourette syndrome is primarily a disorder that is biological and genetic in nature, it occurs equally across all socioeconomic groups—poor, middle class, and the wealthy. As of yet there are no known socioeconomic factors that might predispose an individual to developing TS. However, because poor families typically have reduced access to health care, oftentimes TS patients in these families are under- or misdiagnosed. In addition, since anxiety and stressful events are known to increase the severity of tics, it is possible that a child growing up in a stressful environment (i.e., in poverty, surrounded by domestic abuse or unstable family relationships) might have more severe tics than a child growing up in a less stressful environment. However, a stressful environment alone would not cause a non-symptomatic child to develop TS.[11]

• • • • • • • •

SUMMARY

Tourette syndrome occurs in approximately 1 to 2 percent of the world's population, and appears to occur equally across cultures and ethnicities, with a few rare exceptions. One of the most consistent characteristics of TS is that it occurs approximately four times more often in males than in females. Lower socioeconomic status may increase the severity of tics due to the increased incidence of stressful life events, but does not directly cause TS.

Causes of
Tourette Syndrome

We often view medical doctors as being "superhuman," with *their power to heal the wounds and diseases that afflict everyday citizens. However, doctors are human beings just like the rest of us, and even they can be afflicted by serious medical conditions.*

Doctors can even have Tourette syndrome (TS). For example, Dr. Lance Turtle is a doctor who specializes in infectious diseases at the Royal Liverpool University Hospital. Lance was born in London, England, and was brought up in a normal, middle-class family. He started showing signs of tics at the age of four when he began letting out sudden and peculiar high-pitched shrieking sounds. This particular tic lasted for a few months, and then disappeared on its own. A few years later, he started to jerk his head to one side or the other. This became embarrassing not only to Lance, but to the administrators and teachers at his school—at one point his choirmaster suggested that Lance be put on tranquilizers so as not to look odd during choir performances. Lance has one sister who never exhibited tics, and Lance's vocal tics were never obscene in nature. At the age of 13, Lance went to a boarding school, where he continued his head twitches and also started to make sudden gulping noises. Often Lance could feel "premonitions" or "sensations" of these tics about to occur, and the only way to relieve these feelings was to carry out the tic—but often as soon as the tic was performed, that sensation would almost instantly resurface. Lance was bullied frequently at school, and he would try to suppress his tics or would become anxious about having them, which seemed to make the tics worse. By the time Lance was in his mid-teens, he and his family had begun counseling in order to better cope with the tics.

After Lance finished boarding school and went off to college, his tics (especially the vocal tics) decreased in frequency, but never went away completely. Because of the reduced intensity of his tics, Lance was able to become more confident and make lasting friendships with others. Lance excelled academically, and went on to earn both an M.D. and a Ph.D. degree. While in medical school, one of his professors, an expert in the field of tic disorders, diagnosed Lance with TS. As he grew older and increased his knowledge about TS, Lance (now Dr. Turtle) became more able to recognize situations that made his symptoms better or worse.

Lance finds that his tics get worse if he talks about them or is about to be in a situation where he would prefer a tic not to occur (such as giving a lecture to medical students), and he finds that his tics disappear when he concentrates deeply on an activity he is doing, such as rock climbing. He also is less self-conscious about his tics and accepts them as part of who he is as a person, which helps reduce the frequency of his tics. As with many TS patients, Lance has some symptoms of OCD and ADHD—he often obsesses about whether he locked his car, he has a short attention span, and is often "fidgety." Lance married another doctor and is currently a successful scientific researcher and physician residing in the Liverpool area of England.[1]

GENETIC FACTORS

Although Tourette syndrome has many psychological and social impacts, it is a disorder rooted in genetics and biology. TS patients often have relatives (i.e., siblings, parents, children) with the same or similar disorder, which has led scientists to believe that TS has a strong genetic basis.[2] Studies on identical

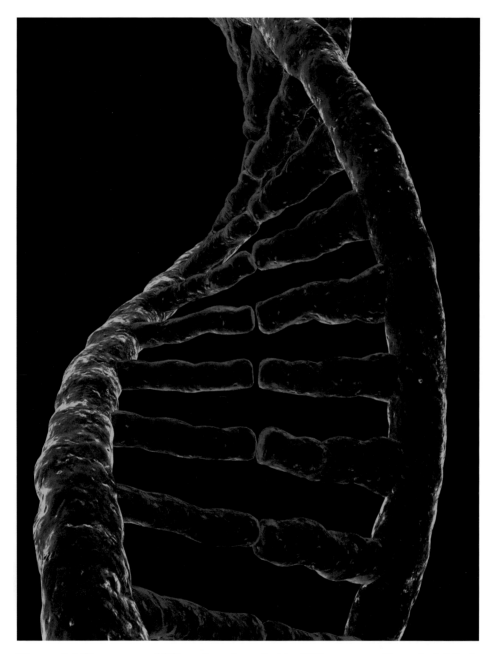

Figure 4.1 The causes of TS are largely rooted in DNA, our genetic material that has a double-helix shape. DNA consists of millions of molecules that form the genetic code for all organisms. *(Sebastian Kaulitzki/Shutterstock)*

twins (often called **monozygotic twins** because they arose from a single fertilized egg, or **zygote**, that divided to form two individual fetuses that have identical genetic makeups) have shown that if one twin has symptoms of TS, then there is a 50 to 70 percent chance that his or her identical twin will also have symptoms of TS or other tic disorder. However in fraternal twins (often called **dizygotic twins** because they arose from two separate fertilized eggs and therefore only share about 50 percent genetic similarity), the likelihood of one twin developing symptoms of TS if his or her twin has the disorder is less than 10 percent.[3] Geneticists who study TS have linked the disorder to numerous possible **genes** (sequences of DNA that form the blueprint for the production of specific proteins) that lie on various **chromosomes** (the structures in each cell in our body that contains our DNA). However, due to the high amount of variability in the types and severity of TS symptoms, it is likely that the disorder is not caused by an inheritance of a single mutated gene, but that numerous genes likely cause the disorder.[4]

ABNORMALITIES IN THE CHEMISTRY OF THE BRAIN

Nerve cells in the brain use chemical messengers called neurotransmitters to communicate with one another. One way scientists attempt to determine the precise disturbances in a particular chemical messenger system that might underlie a psychiatric or neurological condition is by examining the response of a patient to a specific type of medication. Many medications that have been developed to treat mental and neurological disorders target a specific neurotransmitter system. For example, **antipsychotic** drugs used to treat schizophrenia typically inhibit the ability of dopamine to bind to its receptors. Many other drugs (such as antidepressants) are designed to alter the way the neurotransmitter serotonin is used as a chemical signal between nerve cells.

There is a fair amount of evidence that nerve cells that use the neurotransmitter dopamine as their chemical messenger are altered in Tourette syndrome.[5] For example, antipsychotic medications that block dopamine receptors tend to alleviate the frequency and intensity of tics, whereas amphetamines, which cause an excess release of dopamine from neurons, make tics worse. Scientists are currently investigating whether in the brains of TS patients there are abnormally high levels of

How Nerve Cells Communicate

In the brain, nerve cells (neurons) carry electrical signals along wire-like nerve fibers called axons. At the end of each axon is a mushroom-shaped nerve ending called a synaptic terminal. Axons in the brain can range from less than a millimeter in length to up to several centimeters. When the electrical signal traveling down the axon reaches the synaptic terminal, it causes chemical messengers (called neurotransmitters) to be released and secreted onto nearby receiving neurons. This junction between a synaptic terminal and a nearby receiving neuron is called a synapse; there are literally billions of synapses in the brain, and each neuron can have as many as 10,000 different synapses on it. After neurotransmitters are released, they diffuse away from the synaptic terminal into the synapse and encounter proteins (called receptors) on the surface of nearby receiving neurons. Receptors are specific proteins that are designed to recognize specific neurotransmitters. When activated by neurotransmitters, these receptors can cause the receiving nerve cell on which they reside to either become activated (so it passes along the electrical signal) or inhibited (so it doesn't pass along the signal). In order for the dopamine being released by neurons, whether they have super-sensitive dopamine receptors, or whether they have too many dopamine-releasing cells in certain parts of the brain.

There is also evidence that the neurotransmitter **serotonin** may be involved in TS. A study of TS patients showed that they had reduced levels of a brain protein called the serotonin transporter, which takes serotonin that has been released by nerve cells and reabsorbs it for future use.[6] Another study showed

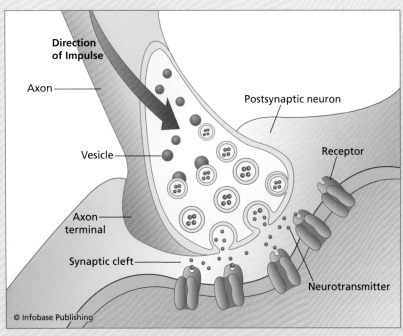

Figure 4.2 Diagram of a chemical synapse within the brain.

nerve to terminate the chemical signal, it reabsorbs the neuro-transmitter back into the synaptic terminal by specialized proteins called transporters, so as to terminate the neurotrans-mitter signal and reuse it for future nerve impulses.

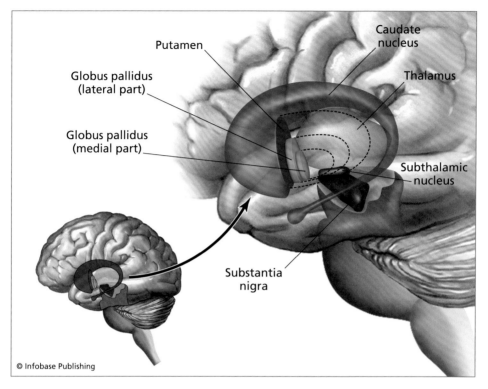

© Infobase Publishing

Figure 4.3 Diagram of brain structures that make up the basal ganglia. Possible malfunctioning of dopamine and/or serotonin systems in these regions is thought to contribute to the symptoms of TS.

that a medication called ondansetron, which inhibits a certain type of serotonin receptor from binding serotonin, can reduce the incidence of tics in TS patients.[7] Serotonin is also highly implicated in the symptoms of OCD, and given the common occurrence of OCD symptoms in TS patients, it is not surprising that this neurotransmitter may contribute to one or both of these disorders.

Nerve synapses that contain serotonin or dopamine are found in high levels in a collection of brain regions known as the **basal ganglia** (see Figure 4.3), which is involved in controlled voluntary movements. Thus, it is highly speculated that a malfunction of this brain region may be responsible for the symptoms of TS.

IMAGING THE TOURETTE SYNDROME BRAIN

Advances in medical technology over the past several decades have given rise to more sophisticated and useful ways to take a "snapshot," or image, of the living human brain (see sidebar). Some of the first brain imaging studies of TS patients, using PET scan technology, showed that various parts of the basal ganglia as well as the cerebral cortex (the wrinkled outermost portion of the brain) were underactive compared to people without Tourette syndrome.[8] Studies using MRI have identified specific regions of the brain, particularly in regions of the cerebral cortex where thinking and planning occur, that become overactive when a person attempts to suppress a tic, as well as when tics are being carried out.[9] Finally, scientists have begun to use recently developed techniques such as morphometry and volumetric MRI to determine subtle structural changes in specific brain regions of TS patients, and some of these studies have shown that certain areas of the basal ganglia are reduced in volume as compared to unaffected people.[10]

THE IMMUNE SYSTEM AND TOURETTE SYNDROME

Once thought to be completely separate entities in the body, the nervous system and the immune system are now believed to be clearly and intricately interconnected. For example, chronic stress—which is processed by the brain—can compromise the immune system and lead to an inability to fight off infections. Another example is when a person has an infection (which activates the immune system), he or she may feel fatigued and lethargic, which is mediated by the brain. There are numerous diseases in which the immune system mistakenly attacks certain parts of the body (including the nervous system) and impairs its normal functioning, instead of serving its normal role in fighting off foreign bacteria and viruses. This type of illness where the immune system attacks a person's healthy tissues and organs is called an **autoimmune disorder.** Examples of autoimmune disorders that affect the nervous system include multiple

Ways to Look at the Living Brain

Brain researchers are constantly developing new and better ways to take a look inside the living human brain and identify possible causes of psychiatric and neurological diseases. One of the most popular types of brain "scans" is the positron emission tomography (PET) scan, where the patient is given an intravenous injection of a mildly radioactive form of water or sugar, which then travels to the brain and can be detected by a PET scanner. Areas of the brain that are active show higher levels of absorption of the radioactive water or sugar than non-active areas, and this allows researchers to determine what brain regions are being activated at a particular moment (i.e., during a tic or tic premonition). Radiolabeled compounds that interact with specific neurotransmitter receptors or other proteins can also be used. However, the drawbacks of this imaging technique include the necessity of exposing the patient to low levels of radioactivity, and the level of detail in the brain scan is somewhat limited.

Another technique used to image the brain is called magnetic resonance imaging (MRI), which captures increases in blood flow to certain parts of the brain when they become more active. Advantages of this technique include the fact that radioactivity is not required, and the level of detail is greater than that afforded by PET, but an MRI can still only

sclerosis and Lou Gehrig's disease, which are characterized by muscle weakness and paralysis.

In the late 1990s Dr. Susan Swedo, a prominent scientist at the National Institute of Mental Health, proposed an evidence-based theory that some patients with TS might also

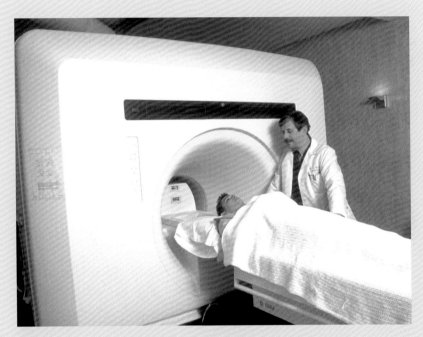

Figure 4.4 A patient undergoing an MRI scan. *(newscom)*

measure changes in brain activity, not activity of brain regions when they are at rest.

In recent years, technology advances have allowed researchers to compare the sizes and volumes of individual brain structures of patients with certain conditions as compared to unaffected individuals. This type of imaging is often referred to as morphometry or volumetric MRI.

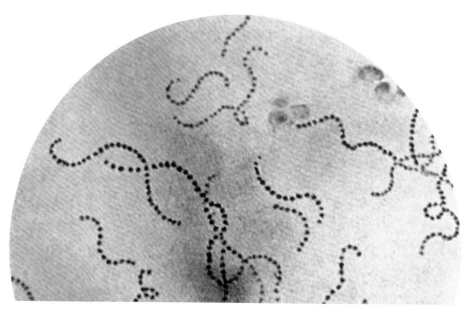

Figure 4.5 Photomicrograph of *Streptoccocus pyogenes* bacteria. *(Centers for Disease Control and Prevention)*

be classified as having a disorder called **pediatric autoimmune neuropsychiatric disorder associated with streptococcal infection (PANDAS).**[11] In this hypothesis, upon becoming infected with a strain of bacteria called **streptococcus pyogenes** (which is the same type of bacteria that causes strep throat)—particularly a subtype of this bacteria called Group A beta-hemolytic streptococci (GABHS)—some children's immune systems react in such a way that it begins to attack not only the streptococcus bacteria, but also the nerve cells in the brain. In Dr. Swedo's original study, she found that there was a strong association between streptococcal infection and the appearance and intensification of symptoms of OCD, TS, or other tic disorder in 50 children. In a follow-up study, it was found that children with OCD, TS, or other tic disorders were much more likely to have had a streptococcal infection three months prior to the onset of their psychiatric and neurological symptoms.[12] In addition, Dr. Swedo showed that the highest probability (an odds ratio of approximately 13 to 1) for developing OCD, TS, or another tic disorder was having multiple streptococcal infections within a 12-month period. However, other studies have since been conducted showing little or no association between streptococcal infection and TS or other tic disorders.[13] Thus, the PANDAS theory, which suggests that there might be an environmental trigger for TS (rather than purely genetic causes), has not been fully confirmed. However, the high level of association between the streptococcal infections and the development of symptoms of OCD, TS, or other tic disorders clearly suggests that further research is needed to confirm this link, and whether preventative treatments might eliminate the development of some cases of TS.

● ● ● ● ● ● ● ●

SUMMARY

Most evidence suggests that Tourette syndrome is a genetic inherited disorder that results in a malfunction of brain regions controlling voluntary movements and the production of sounds and language. Because of the wide variety and severity of symptoms of TS, it is unlikely the disorder is a result of the malfunction of a single gene, but rather multiple genes. Studies with medications have shown that the primary neurotransmitters that mediate the symptoms of TS are dopamine and serotonin. A group of brain structures called the basal ganglia is believed to function abnormally in TS. There is some evidence that TS is an autoimmune disorder brought on or made worse by infections from streptococcal bacteria, but more research is needed to confirm this possibility.

Medical Treatments
for Tourette Syndrome

Sam was six years old when he developed his first vocal tics, *which consisted of sudden chirping sounds like that of a bird. Because Sam was one of the larger kids in his kindergarten class, his classmates would tease him and call him "Big Bird." By the time Sam entered first grade, he developed a motor tic that caused him to suddenly kick one of his feet out in front of him. This led to his classmates calling him the "Kickin' Chicken" after a popular restaurant chain.*

Sam hated his tics and the associated teasing, and found it very hard to make friends. Sam's parents often became frustrated with him, telling him to "stop it with that silly behavior!" When punishments such as taking away TV privileges and giving him time-outs failed to stop Sam's tics, his parents took him to see his pediatrician to find out what was causing these odd behaviors and how stop them. The pediatrician referred Sam to a neurologist, who quickly diagnosed Sam as having Tourette syndrome. The neurologist prescribed a medication called haloperidol, which blocks dopamine receptors and is often used to treat schizophrenia.

The neurologist also referred the family to a psychological therapist to help the family cope with the tics, identify potential triggers, and develop strategies to suppress them. After two weeks of taking the medication, Sam's tics decreased dramatically and occurred only a few times per day. However, the medication made him feel very lethargic and tired all the time, and gave him painful muscle tension in his neck and back. These side effects were severe enough that they caused Sam to fall asleep in class every day, and at recess he could not play any sports because of his muscle aches. So he and his family went back to the neurologist, who prescribed a newer medication called ziprasidone, which got rid of the muscle aches and left Sam only slightly sedated so that he only needed to take a nap when get got home from school. Sam is currently still taking ziprasidone and his symptoms have been reduced by about 75 percent. His is doing very well in school and has made several good friends.

There are numerous options for medical treatment of Tourette syndrome (TS). Drugs that block dopamine receptors in the brain are by far the most commonly used medications, but these medications do not work in all TS patients, and sometimes their side effects are severe enough that the patient has to stop taking them. More recently, advanced neurosurgical techniques have been developed to treat severe cases of TS and those that do not respond to medications. It should be noted, however, that medications or surgical treatment of TS are not cures. Many times tics persist following these treatments, albeit to a much lesser degree. Thus, a comprehensive treatment plan for TS should also include counseling in order to psychologically cope with the illness, educational efforts on the part of the family and teachers, and behavioral therapy.

NEUROLEPTICS

Neuroleptics are a class of medications that act by blocking dopamine receptors, thereby inhibiting the ability of dopamine to transmit chemical signals between neurons. The first neuroleptics were discovered more than 50 years ago, and have traditionally been used to reduce symptoms of schizophrenia, particularly the symptoms of psychosis (hallucinations, delusions, disordered thought patterns, and a loss of touch with reality). Because of their primary use in reducing symptoms of psychosis, neuroleptics are often referred to as antipsychotics. Most neuroleptics reduce the frequency and severity of tics by more than 70 percent.[1] However, most, if not all, of these medi-

Table 5.1 Neuroleptics used to treat Tourette Syndrome

DRUG NAME	DOSE (IN MG/DAY)	COMMON SIDE EFFECTS
aripiprazole	10–20	sedation, headache, nausea, weight gain, akathisia, anxiety, blurred vision
fluphenazine	4–24	sedation, irritability, dysphoria, dystonia, akathisia
haloperidol	0.25–6.0	sedation, dystonia, akasthisia, dysphoria, weight gain, tardive dyskinesia
olanzapine	2.5–20.0	sedation, weight gain, metabolic disturbances
pimozide	1–8	weight gain, akathisia, dystonia, anxiety, depression, tardive dyskinesia
quetiapine	100–600	sedation, weight changes, dizziness, dysphoria
risperidone	0.25–6.0	sedation, dizziness, akathisia, dystonia, depression, headache, OCD
sulpiride	200–1000	sedation, akathisia, depression, weight gain
tiapride	50–150	dysphoria
ziprasidone	5–40	sedation, heart beat irregularities

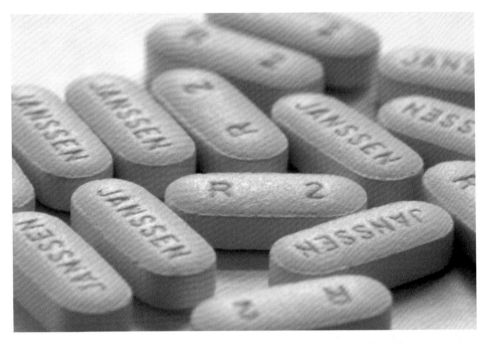

Figure 5.1 Risperidone is a commonly prescribed neuroleptic for the treatment of Tourette syndrome. *(Chris Gallagher/Photo Researchers, Inc.)*

cations have some side effects, and in some people these can be severe enough to force them to discontinue taking the medication. Such side effects include sedation, significant weight gain, irritability, dizziness, headaches, depression and anxiety, **dysphoria** (a strongly unpleasant or uncomfortable mood), **akathisia** (feelings of inner restlessness), **dystonia** (prolonged and often painful muscle contractions that can cause abnormal posture or difficulty moving), and **tardive dyskinesia**. Tardive dyskinesia is a condition characterized by repetitive, purposeless, and involuntary movements that closely resemble the tics exhibited by TS patients; however, tardive dyskinesia is a direct result of prolonged use of neuroleptics. Table 5.1 lists the standard neuroleptics used to treat TS, the dose ranges, and common side effects associated with each.[2]

All of these medications block dopamine receptors. However, some of the more recently developed neuroleptics, such as risperidone, olanzapine, and ziprasidone, also block some types of serotonin receptors, and this additional mode of action is believed to underlie the better treatment outcomes that are typically found with these newer medications.

OTHER MEDICATIONS

Although neuroleptics are the mostly commonly used medications for controlling the frequency and severity of tics, some other medications with varying modes of action (see Table 5.2) also appear to be effective.[3] While these medications have not

Table 5.2 Non-neuroleptics used to treat Tourette syndrome

DRUG NAME	DOSE (IN MG/DAY)	MODE OF ACTION
baclofen	15–30	central nervous system depressant, muscle relaxant
botulinum toxin	75–250 IU*	reduces muscle contractions
clonazepam	0.25–3.0	central nervous system depressant, muscle relaxant
clonidine	0.2–0.4	reduces the activity of the neurotransmitter norepinephrine
guanficine	2–4	reduces the activity of the neurotransmitter norepinephrine
pergolide	0.15–0.45	reduces dopamine release from neurons
tetrabenazine	25–150	promotes the degradation of dopamine

*Because botulinum toxin is a protein (as opposed to smaller molecules like the rest of the drugs listed here), it is measured in International Units (IU).

Figure 5.2 Botulinum toxin (type A), commonly referred to as Botox, is sometimes used to decrease muscle contractions to prevent motor tics, particularly those in the facial muscles. Botox is more commonly used cosmetically to reduce wrinkles in the face. *(Saturn Stills/Photo Researchers, Inc.)*

been as thoroughly tested as the neuroleptics, they do offer hope for improved medications without the numerous undesirable side effects of neuroleptics.

IMMUNE-BASED THERAPIES

The PANDAS theory about the cause of some cases of Tourette syndrome is that it is an autoimmune disorder, where

Nicotine, Marijuana, and Tourette Syndrome

Surprising as it may sound, research has shown that nicotine, the primary psychoactive and addictive substance in tobacco smoke, and delta-9-tetrahydrocannabinol (THC), the main psychoactive ingredient in marijuana smoke, can actually reduce the symptoms of Tourette syndrome. Nicotine, given in the form of a chewing gum or skin patch, has been shown to reduce the frequency of tics in some TS patients.[4] While nicotine was only effective in some patients, a larger reduction in tics was observed when it was combined with the neuroleptic haloperidol.[5] The reasons for this beneficial effect of nicotine are not yet known, and since nicotine is habit forming, many doctors are reluctant to give it to TS patients (who are primarily children). However, the findings indirectly suggest that the neurotransmitter acetylcholine, whose receptors are targeted by nicotine, may play a role in controlling tics.

A study published in the late 1980s showed that in three TS patients, marijuana smoking was associated with a significant reduction in the frequency of tics.[6] A subsequent clinical trial showed that giving TS patients THC in pill form also had beneficial effects in reducing tics.[7] Despite these findings, the use of THC for the treatment of TS has not been actively pursued for numerous reasons, including the possibility of the development of addiction to THC or marijuana, impairments in the development of higher mental capacities since the drug would be given during childhood and adolescence, and the illegal status of marijuana. However, synthetic drugs that mimic the actions of THC might eventually prove to be beneficial for the treatment of TS.

bacterial infections cause the immune system to mistakenly attack nerve cells in the brain. Therefore, drugs targeting the immune system might be beneficial in the treatment of TS. Several studies have shown that intravenous administration of **gamma globulin** (also known as immunoglobulin G, or IgG)—which overloads the immune system with proteins and makes it more difficult for harmful gamma globulins activated by an infection to attack the brain's nerve cells—reduces the severity of tics in some patients.[8] Other drugs that reduce the activity of the immune system, such as the anti-inflammatory drug celecoxib, have been shown to reduce the symptoms of TS.[9] Antibiotics, which kill many types of bacteria, also have been shown to improve symptoms in patients with tic disorders brought on by bacterial infections.[10] However, drugs that suppress the immune system also reduce the ability of the body to fight off newer infections, and therefore long-term use of immune-suppressing drugs is usually discouraged by doctors.

ELECTROCONVULSIVE THERAPY

Electroconvulsive therapy, often abbreviated ECT, is an older, controversial, but still widely used technique to treat various mental conditions such as depression, bipolar (manic-depressive) disorder, and schizophrenia. Through a specialized device (see Figure 5.3), a significant amount of electrical current is applied to the head and passed through the brain, enough so that the patient convulses and has seizures (although muscle relaxants and sedatives are also given prior to the electrical current to reduce this). For reasons that are still unknown, ECT seems to reduce the severity of tics in Tourette syndrome.[11] The ECT treatments must be given at regular intervals (i.e., every few weeks) in order for the treatment to maintain its effectiveness. However, because there is evidence that ECT may cause unwanted side effects, such as memory loss, ECT is only used in severe cases of TS that do not improve with other therapies.

DEEP BRAIN STIMULATION

A more recent advance in the treatment of Tourette syndrome is a neurosurgical procedure called **deep brain stimulation**, or

Rodents Help Us Search for a Cure

Laboratory rodents have been an invaluable asset to the advance of modern medical science. Many treatments for diseases that are used today in humans were initially validated in laboratory rats or mice. In order to test newer treatments, the disease that is being targeted often has to be "modeled," or mimicked, in rodents. For example, through modern genetic engineering, scientists have been able to breed mice whose brains degenerate to the point of death in the same way as it does in Alzheimer's disease. Recently, scientists have reported that the symptoms of Tourette syndrome could be mimicked in rats.[12] In one study, Dr. Jane Taylor at Yale University School of Medicine injected antibodies (proteins produced by the immune system that identify cells to be destroyed by other components of the immune system) from TS patients directly into the brains of laboratory rats, and found that the rats later started to show behaviors that were similar to tics (i.e., repeated twitching of the facial muscles, protrusions of the tongue, etc.).[13] Rats injected with antibodies from healthy individuals did not develop these tic-like symptoms. In another study, mice were genetically engineered to have increased amounts of dopamine secreted by nerve cells, and these mice developed tic-like behaviors.[14] These rodent models of TS will hopefully provide a mechanism by which to test new investigative therapies for the treatment of this disorder.

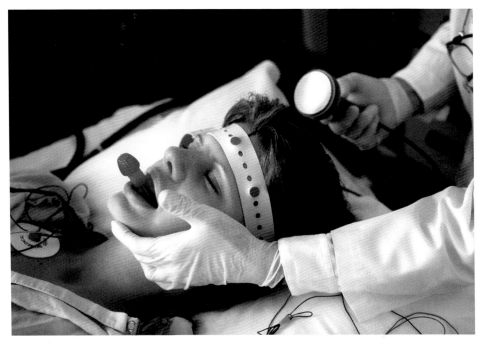

Figure 5.3 A patient undergoing electroconvulsive therapy (ECT). *(Will McIntyre/ Photo Researchers, Inc.)*

DBS. In DBS, while a patient is under anesthesia, a thin metal electrode is inserted into a very precise location of the brain that is thought to be overactive and contributing to the symptoms of TS. The electrode is connected to a device called a pulse generator (similar to a pacemaker used for heart problems) that is implanted under the skin of the chest or back (see Figure 5.4), and small pulses of electrical current are delivered at regular intervals into the target brain region. Despite its name, however, DBS does not actually stimulate the brain—rather, the electrical current emitted by the electrode actually causes nerve cells to shut down. This has the effect of inactivating specific regions of the brain. Since it was first developed, DBS has been used to treat various movement disorders, including Parkinson's disease, and there is evidence that DBS is effective in reducing

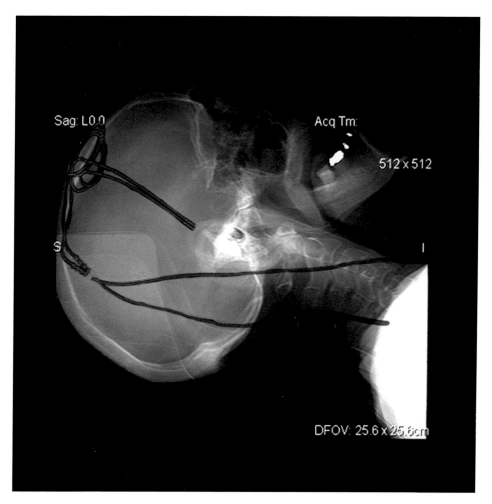

Figure 5.4 Deep brain stimulation involves the implantation of an electrode into a specific brain region (in this diagram, the thalamus). The electrode is connected to a lead (a wire) that exits the skull and extends down the neck to connect to a pulse generator, which uses batteries to deliver regular controlled pulses of electricity to the specific brain region. *(Medical Body Scans/Photo Researchers, Inc.)*

tics when the electrode is placed in parts of the basal ganglia or a region called the **thalamus**.[15] There are some side effects with DBS, which can include psychological disturbances such as hallucinations, as well depression and compulsive behaviors. These side effects usually can be corrected by adjusting the amount of electrical current delivered through the electrode, or repositioning the electrode slightly. Since DBS involves delicate surgery on the brain and is extremely costly, it is used only in cases of TS that do not respond to medications or ECT.

TRANSCRANIAL MAGNETIC STIMULATION

A less invasive method for stimulating or inactivating specific brain regions is a newly developed technique called **transcranial magnetic stimulation** (TMS). In this procedure a device that produces magnetic fields is positioned next to the head and directed

Figure 5.5 Transcranial magnetic stimulation uses pulses of magnetic waves to excite areas on the surface of the brain without the need for surgery. *(Roi Cohen Kadosh)*

at a portion of the brain, usually a specific region of the cerebral cortex (the outermost wrinkled part of the brain). The pulses of magnetic waves cause the nerve cells in the targeted brain region to become activated. Longer lasting effects are observed when multiple magnetic stimulations are performed, a procedure known as **repetitive transcranial magnetic stimulation** (rTMS). TMS and rTMS have been shown to be effective therapies for treating disorders such as depression, Parkinson's disease, and migraines. A few studies have shown that TMS is effective in reducing tics in patients with Tourette syndrome.[16] Advantages of TMS and rTMS are that they cause little or no discomfort to the patient and do not require surgical procedures. However, since TMS and rTMS excite nerve cells, excessive stimulation can result in seizures, particularly in people with epilepsy. In addition, TMS and rTMS are inherently limited by the fact that the magnetic pulses do not appear to penetrate deeply into the brain and are only effective in stimulating areas near the surface of the brain. Since the basal ganglia is a collection of small, deep brain structures that are involved in the generation of tics, it unlikely TMS or rTMS could be used to target these deeper regions.

PSYCHOSURGERY

In the most severe cases of Tourette syndrome, when the tics result in the patient injuring his or herself or others (called malignant Tourette syndrome), more drastic surgical procedures are sometimes employed. One of these procedures is called **psychosurgery** and involves either removing or intentionally damaging specific brain regions with hopes that in doing so, the injurious behaviors will be reduced or eliminated. There are reports that removing the nerve fibers that connect the left and right parts of the brain called the **cingulum** help reduce the severity of harmful tics.[17] This procedure, called a **cingulotomy,** is often accompanied by side effects that are common after any

head surgery, including nausea, vomiting, headaches, and seizures. Removal or destruction of parts of the thalamus (called a
thalamotomy) has also been reported to significantly reduce tic
severity. Although cingulotomy and thalamotomy are not without some side effects, such as temporary loss of speech, confu-
sion, and difficulty moving certain parts of the body, they are
less "barbaric" than older types of psychosurgery that removed
or damaged larger portions of the front part of the brain (called
the **frontal cortex**).[18] These **lobotomies**, sometimes called **leucoto-
mies**, tended to produce severe personality changes and diminished mental capabilities, and are rarely used today.

• • • • • • • •

SUMMARY
The first type of medical treatment usually given to a person
after he or she has been diagnosed with Tourette syndrome is
a neuroleptic, which is a drug that blocks dopamine receptors
and reduces the severity of tics. However, there are numerous
undesirable side effects with neuroleptics, which often force
the patient to change his or her dose or medication type. Other
medications such as sedatives, muscle relaxants, or drugs that
inhibit the actions of the neurotransmitter norepinephrine
are also used. There is some evidence that both nicotine and
marijuana are effective in reducing tics, but because of the
addictive properties of these drugs and the social controversy
that surrounds their use as medicines, they are not frequently
prescribed as medical treatments. Antibiotics or drugs that suppress the activity of the immune system are effective in some
patients. When these types of treatments fail to reduce the
symptoms of TS, most often in more severe cases of TS, more
aggressive approaches to reducing tics can be taken, including
electroconvulsive therapy, deep brain stimulation, transcranial
magnetic stimulation, or psychosurgery.

It should be noted that the medical therapies for Tourette syndrome described above are rarely used alone. The most beneficial and comprehensive approach to treating this disorder would also include behavioral therapies, addressing symptoms of other psychiatric conditions that often co-occur with TS, such as OCD and ADHD, and psychological counseling for coping with the disorder as well as education of the patient and his or her family, friends, and educators.

Behavioral Therapies for Tourette Syndrome

Brian was eight years old when he first started experiencing motor tics, including repeatedly rolling his eyes and wrinkling his nose. These tics later evolved into repetitive outward movements of his arms. By the time Brian was 10, he had developed a vocal tic characterized by a low gurgling noise from the back of his throat. All of his tics were preceded by typical premonitory urges that a tic was about to occur. One day Brian exhibited an episode of both types of tics during a singing performance at his elementary school, which embarrassed Brian as well as his parents, who were in the audience. Soon after that, Brian's mother took him to a neurological clinic where he was diagnosed with Tourette syndrome.

Brian was distressed by his tics, especially by the fact that he felt helpless in controlling them and could not predict when they were going to occur. Playing football or video games with his friends seemed to make Brian's tics occur less frequently, but they increased when he was put in stressful situations, such as the singing performance. Brian's neurologist introduced him to Ms. Anderson, a trained behavioral therapist who specialized in helping children minimize their tics. Ms. Anderson then initiated a type of therapy called habit reversal therapy, or HRT. First, Brian was asked to describe in detail one of his tics, and he chose to focus on the involuntary movement of his right arm outward from his body. Ms. Anderson then asked Brian to say the letter "t" every time his arm tic occurred. If he forgot to say the letter, the *therapist reminded him to do it. Brian was instructed to continue this practice at home, and his mother was instructed to give him reminders when she noticed him having a tic and not saying the letter "t." They both were also given an assignment of having 30-minute monitoring periods several days a week, during which the two of them would write down on a piece of paper every time the tic occurred. Brian was also given a hand counter to carry with him at all times so that he could push a button to tally how many of his arm tics occurred per day. Ms. Anderson then asked Brian's mother to videotape Brian during one of the monitoring periods to document the tics and whether Brian was saying the letter "t" and writing it down.*

After a week, Brian and his mother went back to see Ms. Anderson to compare how well the two of them were documenting Brian's tics, and Ms. Anderson showed Brian a videotape of him performing his arm tic so he had an idea of what it looked like from the outside. Ms. Anderson then introduced the technique called a competing response, or CR. Whenever Brian felt a premonitory urge of his arm about to move outward away from his body, Brian was to intentionally force his arm in the opposite direction close to his body for a full minute, or until the premonitory urge was gone. He was also supposed to do this CR even after an arm tic occurred, to strengthen the habit of doing so. Brian was to do this at home as well during his 30-minute monitoring sessions, and practice it as much as he could at other times as well. Brian's mother rewarded Brian with a $20 bill for every two weeks Brian successfully did his CR homework assignments. By the end of two months of treatment, the frequency of Brian's arm tics had dropped in half, and Brian began to feel improved self-confidence in his newfound ability to be more in control of his tics. With the help of Ms. Anderson and his mother, Brian began to start practicing habit reversal therapy on his eye rolling, nose twitching, and vocal tics.

In addition to the medication and surgical therapies, the treatment of Tourette syndrome also frequently involves some form of behavioral therapy to further reduce tics and help the patient feel more in control of them. Behavioral therapies are needed for several reasons. First, the unpleasant side effects of neuroleptics and other medications used to treat TS result in many patients partially or totally refraining from taking their medication. In addition, our knowledge of the long-term effects of taking neuroleptic or other medications during childhood and adolescence (when the brain and body continue to develop on a daily basis) is incomplete, and many parents worry about possible negative effects the medications might have on the development of their child. Third, both medication and surgical therapies can be costly and unaffordable to many families. Thus, behavioral therapies are valuable assets for use in reducing tics.

MASSED PRACTICE

Massed practice was one of the first types of behavioral therapy for treating Tourette syndrome. It involves the patient purposely, rapidly, and repeatedly performing a certain tic (such as flinching an arm or facial muscle) for a specific time period (such as 30 minutes) interspersed with a shorter time for rest. This process is repeated numerous times and eventually the muscle groups that are involved in executing the tic become fatigued to a point where the tic can no longer be executed, either voluntarily or involuntarily. The inability to execute the tic is a relief to the patient, and in theory, not performing the tic becomes habitual rather than actually performing it. Most studies analyzing the effectiveness of massed practice have shown that it can be beneficial for some patients, but in others can actually make tics worse.[1] Currently, massed practice is not commonly employed as a behavioral therapy for TS.

OPERANT CONDITIONING

The term **operant conditioning** refers to the act of a person performing a task whose consequences increase the likelihood that the task will be performed again. For example, if putting a quarter in a slot machine produces $5 in quarters every time the lever is pulled, the person will likely continue to pump quarters into this "lucky" slot machine. In the context of Tourette syndrome, time periods where a child does not exhibit any tics are rewarded with, for example, a toy or TV privileges (this practice is also sometimes referred to as **contingency management**). In addition, when tics are performed, they are punished. The hypothesis is that the child will enjoy the consequences of being tic-free and avoid the consequences of performing a tic. As with the massed practice, however, most evidence suggests that this type of behavioral therapy does not reduce the frequency of tics.[2] However, when a child is praised by a family member or therapist for adhering to another type of successful behavioral therapy, such as habit reversal therapy, this does seem to have a positive effect on the child and his or her motivation to continue with the therapy.

STRESS AND ANXIETY REDUCTION

It is well known that tics are worsened by psychological stress and anxiety.[3] So, various strategies have been developed to assist Tourette syndrome patients in minimizing stress and anxiety, and these strategies are often used as behavioral therapies to help in the reduction of tics. These strategies are involved **relaxation training**, which consists of the following techniques.

- **Deep breathing exercises.** These typically entail having the TS patient wear loose clothing and sit or lie comfortably, place one of his hands on his chest and the other on his stomach, and slowly inhale through the nose or pursed lips (to slow the rate of air intake). Correct deep breathing can be felt by the stomach expanding, because deep breathing is most effective when the diaphragm contracts and causes the stomach to expand, rather than the rib cage expanding. The patient then slowly exhales, rests, and repeats this process. The result is a reduction in feelings of stress and anxiety, which in turn reduces the frequency of tics.

- **Progressive muscle relaxation.** In this technique, the patient lays down in a comfortable place and takes a few deep breaths (as described above). Soft music may also be played to help the person relax. The patient is then instructed to tense (or constrict) specific muscle groups

Figure 6.1 Relaxation training such as deep breathing, progressive muscle relaxation, and guided imagery are done while sitting or lying in a quiet, comfortable place. *(Phanie/Photo Researchers, Inc.)*

for a few seconds and then relax them. This is typically done in a specific sequence, such as starting with the hands, then the arms, shoulders, neck, and head, and then down the chest and stomach to the legs and the feet. These muscle tension relaxation sequences have the effect of causing a deeper state of relaxation, and therefore reduce stress and anxiety.

- **Guided imagery.** This type of relaxation technique involves the patient lying in a quiet, comfortable place with his or her eyes closed, and a therapist (sometimes

Decaf, Please

In addition to the many behavioral therapies that are used to help control tics, there are lifestyle changes an individual can make that may further reduce the symptoms of Tourette syndrome. These include avoiding or learning coping skills to deal with them. Yet another thing that a TS patient can do to reduce his or her tics is avoid the consumption of stimulants such as caffeine. In a report by Drs. Richard Davis and Ivan Osorio of the University of Kansas Medical Center, these physicians found that two children who had moderate symptoms of TS became completely tic-free by discontinuing an allergy medication that contained pseudoephedrine (a stimulant) and/or eliminating caffeinated beverages and chocolate from their diets.[4] After several months, the children began to drink caffeinated beverages again and their tics re-emerged. Other stimulants, such as methylphenidate (Ritalin) and cocaine, also make tics worse.[5] However, when TS and ADHD are diagnosed in the same person, Ritalin appears to have beneficial effects on the symptoms of both disorders. Clearly, however, not all even an audio tape) guides the patient through a series of relaxing mental images such as meadow, forest, or beach. Often a naturalistic sound recording, such as that of an ocean or gentle stream, is used to help the person focus on the images. The result is a calmed, relaxed state that helps reduce the frequency of tics.

Studies of relaxation training techniques have shown that they can reduce the frequency of tics by approximately 30 percent.[6]

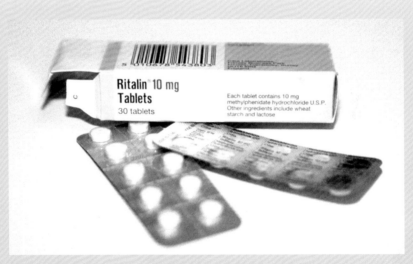

Figure 6.2 Stimulants such as the caffeine in coffee and the medication Ritalin often make tics worse. However, in TS patients who also have ADHD, Ritalin can actually reduce the severity of tics. *(Tracy Dominey/Photo Researchers, Inc.)*

tics can be completely eliminated by avoiding caffeine or stimulants—unfortunately, this type of success tends to be more the exception than the norm.

HABIT REVERSAL THERAPY

Currently, the most widely used and most effective behavioral treatment of Tourette syndrome is called **habit reversal therapy** (HRT).[7] This therapy was originally created by Drs. N. Azrin and R. Nunn in the early 1970s.[8] Prior to initiating HRT, the child and therapist usually create a **tic hierarchy**, where individual tics are rated from 1 to 10 based on how bothersome or distressing they each are. The therapist can then focus on the most distressing tic, followed by less distressing tics.

The first phase of HRT is **awareness training,** which is based on the premise that increased self awareness of tics will create better self-control. First, a TS patient verbally describes his or her tics to the therapist and performs them intentionally by mimicking them. The patient is also asked to sit in front of a mirror so that he or she can observe what the tic looks like. The patient is then trained to make some sort of response (such as the saying of a letter or word) every time a tic occurs. The patient may also be required to keep a written log of his or her tics. The therapist will also train one of the child's parents to take note of when a tic occurs and alert the patient if he or she does not notice it themselves (often tics are performed so frequently throughout the day the TS patient may not be aware of when they happen). A second part of awareness training is teaching the TS patient to identify both the sensations of the premonitory urges that precede tics and the types of situations (i.e., feeling anxious or stressed) when tics are most likely to occur.

Following awareness training, a second phase of HRT begins that is called **competing response** (CR) training. Here, the TS patient is trained to perform a behavior that is opposite to the tic behavior. In the case of Brian at the beginning of this chapter, one of his tics was to flinging his arm outward from his body. The therapist then trained him that as soon as he felt a premonitory urge that the tic was about to occur, he was to perform a CR by purposely pulling his arm inward toward his body. CRs are fairly successful at controlling tics, but if a child finds that his or her tic is too uncontrollable, he or she may be trained to merely minimize the tic (rather than completely eliminate it), or "morph" or "shape" the tic so it looks like a more normal action. For example, if Brian were unable to prevent his arm tic from occurring, after he had already flung his arm outward he would brush back his hair so as to have the appearance that the behavior was intentional in the first place. In other words, the goal is to "disguise" the tic until the patient is more able to control it.

Each CR developed is unique to a specific tic, so if a TS patient has multiple types of tics (as most do), the therapist may repeat the HRT process until each of the tics listed on the tic hierarchy is addressed. To date, HRT has proved to be the most successful behavioral therapy in treating TS, with reductions in the frequency of tics of up to 96 percent.[9]

• • • • • • • •

SUMMARY

Various behavioral therapies have been developed over the years for treating Tourette syndrome without the use of medications or surgery. Some types of therapy, including massed practice and operant conditioning, do not appear to be effective. Others, including stress and anxiety reduction, habit reversal therapy, and avoidance of stimulants seem to be more effective. Unfortunately, to date none of these behavioral therapies are able to completely eliminate tics in all patients, and most often combining a behavioral therapy with a medication such as a neuroleptic is the most effective method for eliminating the symptoms of TS.

Psychiatric Disorders Associated with Tourette Syndrome

Ben was five years old when his tics first started to occur, which primarily consisted of excessive blinking of his eyes. When Ben was nine, he started to experience troublesome thoughts of hurting his older brother Chad, with whom he was very close. Frequently throughout the day an image of hitting his brother with a baseball bat would unexpectedly and repeatedly pop into Ben's head.

These thoughts were very distressing to Ben because of his closeness with his brother, and that Ben was a well-behaved and mildmannered child. These thoughts caused Ben a great deal of anxiety, and he began to wonder why he was having these thoughts, and that if he continued to have them he might actually act them out. Eventually, Ben figured out a way to get these thoughts out of his head once they occurred—he would intentionally blink his eyes rapidly 10 times in a row to make the thought disappear. Ben found that this technique seemed to work, which had the overall effect of increasing his eye-blinking tic even when he was not trying to intentionally blink his eyes. Ben was horrified at what his parents, brother, and friends might think if he ever revealed that he was having these violent thoughts, so he never mentioned them to anyone.

Eventually, by the time Ben left to attend college, the frequency of his eye-blinking tic had significantly decreased, but he continued to have unwanted violent images pop into his mind, which mainly focused on harming his good friends. Because these thoughts *persisted well beyond college, Ben eventually sought out a psychiatrist to find out why these thoughts continued. The psychiatrist told Ben the thoughts were symptoms of obsessive-compulsive disorder and likely a result of a chemical imbalance in his brain, possibly related to the tics he experienced growing up. Ben was given a prescription for the antidepressant Paxil. After a few months of taking this medication, Ben noticed that the frequency of these bothersome thoughts diminished, and even when they did occur, they did not provoke as much anxiety as they did before he started to take the medication. Today, although Ben still has an occasional unwelcome thought about harming a friend or loved one from time to time, he is able to easily dismiss these thoughts as nonsense and "chemical noise" within his brain, and they provoke little or no anxiety.*

Although symptoms of Tourette syndrome can occur by themselves, frequently TS is accompanied by symptoms of other psychiatric disorders, including attention-deficit/hyperactivity disorder (ADHD), obsessive-compulsive disorder (OCD), learning difficulties, depression, anxiety, disruptive behavior, and substance abuse.[1] The occurrence of more than one psychiatric (or other medical) disorder in the same person is called **comorbidity**. Approximately 90 percent of patients with TS also suffer from symptoms of other psychiatric disorders.[2] In this chapter, the psychiatric disorders most commonly associated with TS will be discussed, as will the impact of the symptoms of these disorders on the severity of TS, and treatment options available.

ATTENTION-DEFICIT/HYPERACTIVITY DISORDER

Attention-deficit/hyperactivity disorder (ADHD) is the most common co-occurring psychiatric disorder in people with Tourette syndrome.[3] Approximately 60 percent of TS patients also have symptoms of ADHD.[4] The symptoms of ADHD include inability to focus or concentrate, acting impulsively, difficulties with organization, and may include hyperactivity. For example, a person with ADHD becomes easily distracted and may have difficulty reading just a few sentences in a book without his or her mind wandering elsewhere. Another person with ADHD may be hyperactive and always "on the go," and may also act on impulse, not giving thorough thought to the consequences of his or her behaviors. Like TS, the symptoms of ADHD usually emerge during childhood or adolescence. Because over half of TS patients also have symptoms of ADHD, the prevalence of ADHD among TS patients is higher than that found in the general population.[5]

Why do Tourette syndrome and ADHD co-occur so frequently? One possible theory may lie within the genetic nature of these disorders, with the hypothesis that the same genetic abnormalities that produce symptoms of TS are also responsible for ADHD. There is recent scientific evidence to show that the brains of TS patients with co-occurring ADHD are indeed different from those of TS patients without ADHD.[6] For example, using volumetric brain imaging techniques such as MRI, scientists have found that certain regions of the basal ganglia, such as the caudate nucleus, are smaller in boys aged eight to nine with TS and ADHD as compared with boys with TS alone in this same age group.[7] As a result, some scientists suggest that patients with TS and co-occurring ADHD should receive a separate diagnosis than those patients with TS but without co-occurring ADHD.[8]

Most children with ADHD are treated with mild stimulants, such as methylphenidate (Ritalin) or **Adderall** (a mixture of various forms of amphetamines), which paradoxically have a calming effect and allow for improved concentration. However, stimulants such as caffeine or Ritalin tend to make tics worse. So how would one treat a TS patient with co-occurring ADHD? Most scientific studies to date have found that Ritalin is an effective treatment for children and adolescents with co-occurring TS and ADHD, and that in these patients Ritalin does not make tics worse.[9] These findings also lend support that TS alone

The Paradox of Treating Hyperactivity with Stimulant Medications

If a child is hyperactive and can't sit still or focus his or her attention for more than a few minutes, common sense would indicate that the last type of medication one would want to give the child is a stimulant such as Ritalin or Adderall, as this would seemingly make the problem much worse. However, Ritalin and related stimulants such as Adderall appear to be quite effective in reducing symptoms of ADHD, such as hyperactivity and an inability to concentrate. Scientists are still not quite certain how a stimulant would have a calming effect on a person with ADHD, but they theorize that people with ADHD have a chemical imbalance of dopamine in their brains, particularly in regions such as the frontal cortex, which is involved in impulsivity and attention focusing. Scientists hypothesize that drugs like Ritalin and Adderall correct this imbalance of dopamine.[10] However, in people without ADHD, drugs such as Ritalin may produce hyperactivity and even addiction, because these people have a normal functioning of their dopamine systems, and therefore these medications affect their brains differently than they affect people with ADHD. There is increasing evidence of misuse, abuse, and addiction to Ritalin and Adderall by people without ADHD who use them as a substitute for caffeine to stay awake late at night for studying or socializing. This may lead to problems with the misuse of other stimulants, such as cocaine and amphetamines, later in life.[11]

and TS with co-occurring ADHD may be two separate disorders with various differences in the brain that make the two groups respond so differently to Ritalin. However, because stimulants such as Ritalin can cause anxiety, they are not commonly prescribed for TS patients with co-occurring anxiety disorders.

OBSESSIVE-COMPULSIVE DISORDER

Obsessive-compulsive disorder (OCD) has two main groups of symptoms—**obsessions**, which are repetitive, intrusive, and unwanted thoughts or mental images that lead to behavioral **compulsions**, which are attempts at neutralizing the unwanted thoughts by performing repetitive acts to the point where they interfere with the person's normal functioning. For example, a person with OCD might have a fear of contamination by germs, and that after touching something harmless, such as a pen or telephone, he is struck with overwhelming anxiety about becoming infected with a deadly bacteria or virus, which compels him to wash his hands repeatedly, sometimes several hundred times per day. People with OCD realize that their obsessions and compulsions are senseless, but have extreme difficulty controlling them. The compulsions or obsessions are often so distressing and time consuming that they significantly interfere with the person's normal daily function. A subset of people with OCD appear to suffer from "pure obsessions"—that is, they have repetitive, intrusive, unwanted thoughts, such as images of harm toward a loved one, blasphemous thoughts about God (if the person is religious), or sexually inappropriate thoughts.

It has been estimated that approximately 50 percent of people with Tourette syndrome exhibit symptoms of OCD at some point in their lifetime.[12] The precise incidence of OCD in TS patients is difficult to determine, however, because people who suffer from OCD seldom report their unwanted or repugnant thoughts for fear they might be perceived as dangerous or crazy.

Figure 7.1 Excessive hand washing to overcome the fear of germs and contamination is a common symptom of OCD. *(TheSupe87/Shutterstock)*

In addition, some children show signs of "normal" compulsions, such as arranging all of their stuffed animals in particular order prior to going to bed, but this would only be classified as a pathological consumption if the child were doing so in an attempt to neutralize an irrational fear.

Unlike the symptoms of Tourette syndrome, which tend to dissipate as the adolescent enters adulthood, the symptoms of OCD may persist for many years to come. The majority of people with OCD have obsessions and compulsions that revolve around fear of contamination, becoming ill, or harm coming to a loved one. However, in patients with co-occurring OCD and TS, the obsessions tend to be of a sexual, religious, or aggressive theme, and in these patients there appears to be less severe feelings of anxiety provoked by these obsessions than in people with OCD alone.[13] In addition, the obsessions experienced by TS patients with OCD may also be of a "sensory" nature regarding the part(s) of the body affected by the tic, such as an urge to use that body part to commit an act that they find appalling.[14] Often a patient with both TS and OCD may attempt to disguise their compulsions as part of their tics—for example, a teenager who has an eye-blinking tic will intentionally blink his eyes five times every time he has an unpleasant thought or image enter his mind in an attempt to "neutralize" or get rid of the thought.

Treatment of OCD in Tourette syndrome patients is similar in nature to that used for treating OCD in children without TS. One of the most common approaches is called **exposure plus response prevention**, in which a child is instructed to think about something related to their obsessions, which provokes feelings of anxiety, and then the therapist prevents the child from being able to perform the compulsion that he or she normally engages in to neutralize the anxiety provoked by the obsessive thought. Repeated use of this procedure allows the child to learn, with repeated training, that the compulsion need not be performed in order to rid the mind of the obsessive thought, and that the presence of the thought (such as the harming of a loved one) does not mean that the content of the thought will actually happen. In addition, children with OCD can also undergo some form of cognitive therapy for their obsessions, which trains the child to reappraise the anxiety-provoking thought and dismiss it as nonsense, rather than obsess and worry over it.

In addition to the behavioral therapy approaches, often medications such as antidepressants (i.e., Zoloft, Prozac, or Paxil) are used to reduce the anxiety provoked by the obsessions, as well as the frequency of the obsessions themselves. The type of antidepressant that works best for symptoms of OCD are the **selective serotonin reuptake inhibitors** (SSRIs), which block the ability of neurons to reabsorb the neurotransmitter serotonin after it has been released at a synapse, which has the result of producing excess serotonin levels outside the neurons. Approximately 40 to 60 percent of people who take an SSRI show significant improvement in their OCD symptoms within a few weeks.[15] However, SSRIs are not very effective in reducing tics, and are therefore sometimes are combined with neuroleptics to control the symptoms of both OCD and Tourette syndrome.

DEPRESSION

Depression is common among people with Tourette syndrome, occurring in as much as 75 percent of these patients.[16] Symptoms of depression in adults include prolonged sadness, a loss of pleasure or interest in activities, eating or sleeping habit changes, and frequent thoughts of death or dying. However, in children symptoms of depression may manifest as irritability or anger. Depression is not just the temporary "blues" one feels after having a bad day or breaking up with a boyfriend or girlfriend. Symptoms of depression are severe enough that they interfere with a person's normal daily functions.

In Tourette syndrome, depression is often caused by the demoralizing nature of tics. Children or adolescents with tics often tend to be perceived as "different" or "freaks," are often bullied, and are themselves extremely frustrated with their inability to control their tics and feeling different from their fellow students. TS patients often have trouble making friends, which makes them feel socially isolated. All of these may lead a person with TS to become clinically depressed, which has the overall effect of making tics worse.

Treatment of depression in TS patients is similar to treating depression in people without Tourette syndrome. Many times psychotherapy is used to help children with TS feel less demoralized and isolated. Antidepressants such as Zoloft, Prozac, or Paxil can also be used to reduce the symptoms of depression. Typically, reducing the symptoms of depression also results in a reduction in the severity of tics.

ANXIETY

There are many forms of pathological anxiety, such as phobias (irrational fears of objects, ideas, or situations), generalized anxiety (excessive general feelings of worry), OCD, and **posttraumatic stress disorder** (PTSD), and several others. In people with Tourette syndrome, there is a higher rate of social anxiety and phobias (such as public speaking or public performances) and separation anxiety (such as the anxiety caused by being away from one's parents) than in the general population.[17] This is not surprising, given the social stigma that comes with TS and the protective feelings of being around one's parents and family members who understand TS better than the population at large. Social and separation anxiety in TS is usually treated with psychotherapy and improving the coping skills of the child with TS. Occasionally, antianxiety medications such as Valium or Xanax might be prescribed in more severe cases of anxiety associated with TS. Both types of therapies relieve the feeling of anxiety and can improve the symptoms of TS.

LEARNING DIFFICULTIES

People with Tourette syndrome often exhibit learning difficulties.[18] This is not due to lower IQ levels in patients with TS, since children with TS actually tend to have higher IQs than those of the general population. Rather, the learning difficulties experienced by TS patients are likely a result of their inability to concentrate and focus their attention (as a result of accompanying ADHD), or a result of intrusive and unwanted thoughts interfering with the ability to concentrate and focus (as a result of OCD). As such, treatment of the accompanying ADHD or OCD may improve learning skills in TS patients.

DISRUPTIVE BEHAVIOR

Children and adolescents with Tourette syndrome often show behavioral syndromes that can be very problematic. One such behavioral problem is termed **oppositional defiant disorder**, which is characterized by refusing to obey one's parents, blaming others for their own mistakes, impulsivity, explosive outbursts, tantrums, and sudden attacks of physical and emotional rage against parents or other figures of authority. As many as 15 percent of children with TS exhibit symptoms of oppositional defiant disorder, but this may be secondary to the increased incidence of ADHD in TS patients, since approximately 50 percent of children with ADHD alone also have symptoms of oppositional defiant disorder.[19] Regardless of the cause, children with TS and disruptive behaviors can become violent, physically attacking animals and other people, and engaging in antisocial behaviors such as vandalism or arson. These types of behavioral problems associated with TS require intense psycho-therapy, antipsychotic medications, and often imprisonment. Because most of the public, including police and parole officers, and lawyers and jurors, are undereducated about TS and its biological nature, TS patients with severe behavioral problems seldom have their affliction taken into account when being sentenced for crimes committed, or are committed to psychiatric hospitals.[20] Increased education of personnel engaged in all levels of the legal system about TS is needed in order to provide more appropriate treatment for violent TS patients.

Oppositional defiant disorder is extremely stressful to the parents of the afflicted child, and most often parents are ill-equipped in the proper ways to deal with this type of behavior. For example, to avoid an explosive outburst, sometimes a parent may give in to the child's demands, which only reinforces the behavioral problem. Other times parents will overreact harshly to the child's defiant behavior with severe spankings or sending the child to bed without dinner, which can compound the problem by promoting anger and resentment toward the parents. Recent research has shown that parent management training, which teaches parents the appropriate responses to their children's defiant behaviors and techniques to effectively manage them, is effective in controlling oppositional defiant disorder.[21] Such techniques include: positive reinforcement (rewarding children for good behavior rather than permitting bad behavior in order to avoid tantrums), setting clear expectations of what is acceptable behavior and what is not, use of milder punishments such as five- to 10-minute "time-outs" (such as sitting alone in a corner of the room), and creating point systems so that points can be earned for good behavior (and taken away for bad behavior) with the overall goal that accumulation of a certain number of points can be redeemed for special privileges, foods, candy, etc.

SUBSTANCE ABUSE

As mentioned in Chapter 6, both nicotine and marijuana have been reported to decrease tic severity in some Tourette syndrome patients. Therefore, some TS patients who experiment with either smoking cigarettes or marijuana (particularly adolescents) in an effort to relieve their own symptoms may be at increased risk for becoming addicted to cigarettes or marijuana, and may likely have substance abuse problems in adulthood. An increased risk of substance use problems in adult TS patients is especially prevalent in TS patients with co-occurring ADHD, because people with ADHD tend to be impulsive and do not clearly examine the consequences of their actions, such as experimenting with drugs. There are, however, very few in-depth studies on drug use in TS patients and how it affects their likeliness of having drug use problems later in life.

SLEEP PROBLEMS IN TOURETTE SYNDROME

Problems with sleeping are common in patients with Tourette syndrome.[22] Most often patients with TS have trouble falling asleep due to their tics keeping them awake, or due to the wake-promoting effects of stimulants such as Ritalin given to patients with TS and ADHD. Once asleep, TS patients are often restless, tossing and turning and frequently waking up, which results in poor quality of sleep and sleepiness the following day, which can cause irritability and worsening of tics. Sleepwalking is also common in TS. As in people without TS, sleep quality in TS patients is improved if proper dosages of prescription sleep aids such as Ambien or Lunesta are given, and if taking stimulants is restricted to times of the day that are not close to bedtime. However, prescription sleep aids can be habit-forming, and therefore are not recommended to be used on a nightly basis.

Figure 7.2 Difficulty falling asleep is common among people with Tourette syndrome. *(Karen Winton/Shutterstock)*

• • • • • • • •

SUMMARY

The most frequent psychiatric disorders that co-occur with Tourette syndrome are ADHD and OCD. These disorders are most often treated with mild stimulants such as Ritalin (for ADHD) and SSRIs such as Paxil (for OCD). Remarkably, despite the fact that stimulants tend to make the severity of tics worse in TS patients without ADHD, they do not in children with co-occurring TS and ADHD. TS can also be accompanied by significant degrees of depression, anxiety, learning difficulties, sleep problems, and disruptive behavioral problems such as oppositional defiant disorder. Adolescents with TS who smoke cigarettes and marijuana to alleviate the severity of their tics are at increased risk of becoming addicted to these drugs.

Coping Strategies for Tourette Syndrome Patients and Their Families

Recall the description in Chapter 5 of a boy named Sam who had a vocal tic consisting of a chirping sound. Because Sam was about three inches taller than most of his classmates, they teased him by calling him "Big Bird." Sam was bothered by this teasing, and would often become angry at his classmates and tell them to "shut up." Sam told his teacher, Ms. Hawkins, about the teasing, but she would usually dismiss it as "typical school kid behavior." However, after Sam started to develop his motor tic, the teasing and mocking intensified, and Ms. Hawkins began to think something was wrong with Sam. She also noticed that Sam fell asleep at his desk frequently.

At their next parent-teacher conference, Ms. Hawkins learned from Sam's parents that he had Tourette syndrome (TS). Previously she had only heard about the disorder, but never had seen a child with symptoms. Sam's parents brought some pamphlets about TS to the meeting and talked at length about what could be done to reduce the teasing and accommodate Sam's special needs. They also explained that Sam was on a medication that made him sleepy, which was why he often fell asleep at his desk. Since Sam's academic performance was only mediocre, his parents suggested ways to improve his grades by allowing him to take tests after school to give him extra time. In addition, on days when Ms. Hawkins would notice that Sam's tics were fairly severe, she would send him with the attendance sheets to the main office in order to give him a way to release some of his pent up energy and tics without disturbing the class. With regards to the teasing, Ms. Hawkins immediately adopted a classroom policy that anyone caught teasing Sam (or anyone else in the class), would have to write a written apology to the teasing victim and spend an hour after school picking up trash on the playground. After about two weeks, all teasing virtually disappeared, and other teachers at the school adopted similar policies.

Medications, neurosurgery, and behavioral therapies can be very effective in treating Tourette syndrome. Yet even in today's Internet age, the public is still largely undereducated about TS. As a result, people afflicted by TS are often subjected to embarrassment, harassment, and bullying, and as a result are often socially isolated, angry, or depressed, which can worsen the symptoms of TS. In addition to medical and behavioral treatments for TS and common psychiatric conditions that often co-occur with this disorder, there are other coping and management strategies that need to be undertaken in order to comprehensively treat this disorder. Such strategies include education of the TS patient and his or her family, friends, and teachers; assessment of comorbid disorders; counseling; and making special accommodations at the child's school.[1] There are also strategies to effectively manage the teasing and bullying to which children with TS are often subjected.

EDUCATION OF THE PARENTS AND FAMILY

Upon receiving word that their child has a diagnosis of Tourette syndrome, the child's parents may experience a wide range of emotions: feeling guilty for haven mistaken the tics for bad behavior and punishing the child, or blaming themselves for the "bad genes" that they have passed on to their child; resenting other parents who have "normal" children and are not confronted with the issues that accompany raising a child with

TS; or feeling relieved because they were suspicious that their child's behavior is not normal and they now have found a medical diagnosis with treatment options for TS. However parents react to the diagnosis, the first strategy parents should use is to educate themselves about TS and ways it is treated. Through reading of books, medical journals, and information from support and advocacy groups such as the Tourette Syndrome Association (TSA), parents become aware that TS is a genetically and biologically based brain disorder, and that the tics are not a result of a psychological problem or attempts at getting attention. Adjusting to having a child diagnosed with TS is a lengthy process and does not occur overnight, so parents must be patient in their efforts to understand their child's disorder.

Since Tourette syndrome is often accompanied by other psychiatric conditions such as ADHD and OCD, parents of an afflicted child will often have to educate themselves about these disorders as well, especially if their child with TS starts to show symptoms such as hyperactivity, inability to concentrate, obsessions, or compulsions.

If the child with Tourette syndrome has siblings, particularly younger brothers, the parents may be struck with fear and worry that the sibling may also at some point begin to show symptoms of TS, since the disorder has a large genetic component and is predominantly found in boys. However, as of yet there are no diagnostic or genetic tests that can predict whether a sibling of a child with TS may actually also develop TS. Siblings of the child with TS may also feel resentment toward both the child and their parents because of the extra attention the afflicted child receives. This should be remedied by parents having one-on-one time with the non-affected sibling, such as going to a sporting event or movie together, to make him or her feel equally important as the child with TS. Parents of a child with TS should make a concerted effort toward educating the child's siblings about TS as a biological disorder and not a psychological problem. Parents should also encourage the non-affected siblings to educate their friends about TS, and to give positive support to the child with TS, since high self-esteem is an important factor in reducing the severity of tics.

EDUCATION OF THE TOURETTE SYNDROME CHILD

Once the child with Tourette syndrome is old enough to understand more complex things like medicine and how the body works, the child should become educated about TS as a medical condition in which his or her tics are mostly uncontrollable. This will allow the child to better understand his or her behavior and become less frustrated with his or her lack of ability to control tics, which will improve self-esteem. It will also allow the child to educate his or her own friends about the disorder to reduce teasing and bullying.

COUNSELING

Counseling is important for both the child with Tourette syndrome as well as his or her family. It improves the education of family members about TS, and teaches all members of the family to provide reassurance and support for the child with TS, which leads to improved self-esteem. Counseling also helps a child with TS improve his or her social skills, such as making and maintaining friendships, making eye contact during conversations, and apologizing when an offensive vocal tic occurs. Children with TS should also be encouraged to join local support groups for youths with TS, which provides reassurance that they are not alone and provides the opportunity to learn other children's skills for coping with TS. Likewise, parents should also seek out support groups for parents of children with TS to learn the parenting skills needed for raising a child with TS.

Figure 8.1 Counseling of the child with Tourette syndrome as well as his or her family is a highly valuable strategy to understand and cope with TS. At-home counseling is particularly useful for younger children who feel safer and less anxious at home than in a counselor's office. *(BSIP/Phototake)*

Support groups can usually be found via advocacy groups such as the Tourette Syndrome Association.

EDUCATION OF TEACHERS AND CHANGES IN SCHOOL ACCOMMODATIONS

Since a diagnosis of Tourette syndrome often comes at an age when the child is in preschool or elementary school, and children of this age typically spend four to six hours per day at school, a child is almost certain to have episodes of tics while at school. Therefore, the parents of a child with TS should make every effort to:

- educate the child's teacher about Tourette syndrome as a genetic and biological disorder
- educate the teacher about the child's specific tics and the lack of control he or she has over them, as well as the harmful consequences of punishing the child if the tics disrupts classroom activities
- have the teacher ignore the child's tics, since the teacher serves as a role model and will help teach the child's classmates to do the same (This can be difficult, since particularly complex motor tics or loud vocal tics—especially those involving obscenities—can easily be disruptive to the class; however, ignoring the tics to the extent possible will reduce the stress placed on the child and therefore reduce the severity of the tics.)
- inform the teacher about what other comorbid conditions the child might have, especially ADHD or OCD, as well as the medications the child is currently taking
- have frequent meetings with the teacher to stay updated on the child's academic performance, tic severity, peer relationships, and social skills

Figure 8.2 Frequent meetings between the parents of a child with Tourette syndrome and his or her teacher are critical for open dialogue and mutual understanding of the child, his or her symptoms, and his or her academic, social, and personal growth. *(AP Images)*

Once a well-informed relationship between the parents of the child with TS and his or her teacher has been established, the teacher also needs to establish a positive relationship with the child. Specifically, the teacher should determine which situations make the child with TS stressed or uncomfortable, such as reading aloud or presenting in front of the class. Allowing the child to be exempt from such activities may be a healthy initial approach to prevent the child's tics from worsening due to the stress of being the center of attention, but the child should gradually be encouraged to participate in such activities in order to develop such skills that will be useful later in life. The bottom line is to encourage the child to do what he or she feels comfortable with, but not to force him or her into doing something he or she would find very stressful.

If the students are old enough to understand, teachers should give the child's classmates information about tics. Perhaps at more advanced ages (i.e., ages 10 and up), the teacher may encourage the child to do an oral report on TS and what it is like to have the condition.

Teachers should also provide frequent feedback to the parents on the child's academic progress and social skills. Teachers can be very good monitors of the progress a child is making in his or her struggle with Tourette syndrome. Dialogue between the teacher and the parents is critical for helping the child with TS succeed academically, socially, and personally.

There are numerous other adjustments in the classroom that can be made for the student with TS and his or her classmates to accommodate the afflicted child. These include:

- Allowing a "tic break," which might entail having the child leave the classroom for a short amount of time, particular if he or she is having a bad episodes of tics. Seating the child near the exit of the room may help in this situation.
- In children with Tourette syndrome and behavioral problems such as ADHD or disruptive behaviors, the same strategies employed at home should also be used in the classroom—positive feedback for good behavior, imposing time-outs for bad or aggressive behavior, and setting and enforcing limits on what is acceptable behavior and what is not.
- Allowing the child with TS extra time to complete his or her work, and perhaps break down the assignment into smaller "chunks," or portions of the assignment, so that the child (particularly those with ADHD) can complete

portions of the work before losing their attention on the task.

• Not imposing time limits on tests. The stress of having to finish a test in a certain amount of time may increase the frequency of the tics, and therefore make it more difficult to complete the test in the allotted time. Untimed tests could be given to the child with TS during recess, lunchtime, or after school.

• When homework is assigned, the child with TS should be allowed to do his or her work in a stress- and distraction-free environment, and should be given positive feedback or desired privileges (such as watching TV or playing video games) once all the homework is completed.

• Allowing the use of a laptop computer. Since many tics involve involuntary movements of the hands and arms, the child with TS may exhibit poor handwriting, and therefore the use of a computer for writing assignments may be less stressful.

COPING WITH TEASING AND BULLYING

Teasing and bullying of other children due to differences in appearance, skin color, speech impediments, mental or physical disability, or social status is common in schools, ranging from elementary school on up through high school. **Bullying** is defined as the repeated intentional insulting, threatening, name-calling, humiliating, or even physically harming of a child by another person, most often a child who is older with a larger physical size and higher social status (i.e., a bigger sixth-grade kid picking on a smaller "nerdy" third-grader). Bullying can be direct, as given by the examples above, or indirect, as exemplified by spreading false rumors about the victim or ignoring his or her existence.

Figure 8.3 Bullying of children with Tourette syndrome can be psychological, physical, or both. *(Mandy Godbeheart/Shutterstock)*

The bizarreness of tics in Tourette syndrome often causes school children to think people with TS are different, which provides them with an easy opportunity to tease or bully the child with TS. During the fragile years of childhood, this bullying and teasing can cause lasting psychological scars. In the short term, they can result in increased stress and anxiety, fear of going to school, withdrawal from social situations, nightmares, poor performance in school, and low self-esteem, all of which can worsen the severity of tics. Prolonged bullying can lead to depression, self-harm, or even suicide. In the event of a severe physical attack, the child with TS may suffer from symptoms of post-traumatic stress disorder (PTSD), which is characterized by flashbacks of the traumatic event; avoidance of locations, places, or people associated with the attack; and heightened levels of anxiety.

Parents of a child with TS should be aware that there is a high likelihood that their child will experience some form of teasing or bullying at school. Parents who suspect that their child with TS is being bullied need to listen carefully to the child's reports of bullying and provide positive support. Also, parents should explain why people are bullied, as the child may not understand why he or she is being singled out. They also need to contact the child's teacher and, in more serious instances, the head of the school. Proper ways to resolve

Characteristics of Bullies and their Victims

Below are some common traits of people who bully others, as well as those who are prone to being bullied.[2]

BULLIES	VICTIMS
aggressive tendencies	anxious personality
few close friends	few close friends
psychological need for power and control	sensitive and passive
previous victim of bullying	passive
family problems	easily dominated
feelings of insecurity and jealousy; resentful	bullied at home as well as at school
inability to emphathize with others	has some physical attribute that makes them different

bullying issues are to make the bully apologize face to face or in writing to the victim, punish the bully with school service (e.g., picking up trash), or by detention. In cases of severe physical attacks, the bully may need to be suspended or expelled from school, or even face criminal charges.

• • • • • • • •

SUMMARY

Education of the parents, child with Tourette syndrome, and teachers about the symptoms and biological and uncontrollable nature of tics in TS is of very high importance in reducing the psychological burden of TS. Counseling services and support groups for parents, siblings, and the TS patient should be utilized. Certain accommodations at home and at school, such as extra time for homework or tests, may need to be implemented in order to meet the needs of the child with TS. Parents should also be wary of the high probability that a child with TS will be teased or bullied, and such scenarios must be dealt with promptly and seriously by parents, teachers, and school administrators.

Chapter 1

1. American Psychiatric Association, *Diagnostic and Statistical Manual of Mental Disorders*, 4th ed., text revision (Washington D.C.: American Psychiatric Press, 2002).

2. J. Jankovic, "Tourette Syndrome," *New England Journal of Medicine* 345 (2001): 1184–92.

3. H. I. Kushner, "Medical Fictions: The Case of the Cursing Marquise and the (Re)Construction of Gilles de la Tourette Syndrome," *Bulletin of the History of Medicine* 69 (1995): 224–54.

4. J-M. G. Itard, "Mémoire sur Quelques Fonctions Involuntaires des Appareils de la Locomotion, de la Préhension et de la Voix," *Archives Générales de Médecine* 8 (1825): 385–407.

5. G. Tourette, "Etude sur une Affection Nerveuse Caracaterisée par de l'Incoordination Motrice Accompagenee d'Echolalie et de Coprolalie," *Archives de Neurologie* 9 (1885): 19–42.

Chapter 2

1. A. Ashoori and J. Jankovic, "Mozart's Movements and Behaviour: A Case of Tourette Syndrome?" *Postgraduate Medical Journal* 84 (2008): 313–7.

2. American Psychiatric Association, *Diagnostic and Statistical Manual of Mental Disorders*, 4th ed., text revision (Washington D.C.: American Psychiatric Press, 2002).

3. C. G. Goetz and K. Kompoliti, "Rating Scales and Quantitative Assessment of Tics," *Advances in Neurology* 85 (2001): 31–42.

4. American Psychiatric Association, *Diagnostic and Statistical Manual of Mental Disorders*, 4th ed., text revision (Washington D.C.: American Psychiatric Press, 2002).

5. J. F. Leckman, M. H. Bloch, L. Scahill and R. A. King, "Tourette Syndrome: the Self under Siege," *Journal of Child Neurology* 21 (2006): 642–9.

6. M. M. Robertson, "The Prevalence and Epidemiology of Gilles de la Tourette Syndrome. Part 1: The Epidemiological and Prevalence Studies," *Journal of Psychosomatic Research* 65 (2008): 461–72.

7. M. Y. Cheung, J. Shahed and J. Jankovic, "Malignant Tourette Syndrome," *Movement Disorders* 22 (2007): 1743–50.

8. Ibid.

9. H. I. Kushner, "Medical Fictions: The Case of the Cursing Marquise and the (Re)Construction of Gilles de la Tourette Syndrome," *Bulletin of the History of Medicine* 69 (1995): 224–54.

10. M. M. Robertson, "Tourette Syndrome, Associated Conditions and the Complexities of Treatment. Part 3" *Brain* 123 (2000): 425–62; J. N. Goldenberg, S. B. Brown, and W. J. Weiner, "Coprolalia in Younger Patients with Gilles de la Tourette Syndrome," *Movement Disorders* 9 (1994): 622–5.

11. M. M. Robertson, "The Prevalence and Epidemiology of Gilles de la Tourette Syndrome. Part 1: The Epidemiological and Prevalence Studies," *Journal of Psychosomatic Research* 65 (2008): 461–72.

12. P. J. Hoekstra, M. P. Steenhuis, C. G. Kallenberg and R. B. Minderaa, "Association of Small Life Events

with Self Reports of Tic Severity in Pediatric and Adult Tic Disorder Patients: A Prospective Longitudinal Study," *Journal of Clinical Psychiatry* 65 (2004): 426–31.

13. M. M. Robertson, S. Banerjee, R. Kurlan, D.J. Cohen, J. F. Leckman, W. McMahon, et al., "The Tourette Syndrome Diagnostic Confidence Index: Development and Clinical Associations," *Neurology* 53 (1999): 2108–12.

Chapter 3

1. F. E. Abuzzahab, Sr. and F. O. Anderson, "Gilles de la Tourette Syndrome; International Registry," *Minnesota Medicine* 56 (1973): 492–6.

2. R. D. Bruun, "Gilles de la Tourette Syndrome. An Overview of Clinical Experience," *Journal of the American Academy of Child & Adolescent Psychiatry* 23 (1984): 126–33.

3. M. M. Robertson, "The Prevalence and Epidemiology of Gilles de la Tourette Syndrome. Part 1: The Epidemiological and Prevalence Studies." *Journal of Psychosomatic Research* 65 (2008): 461–72.

4. N. Khalifa and A. L. von Knorring, "Prevalence of Tic Disorders and Tourette Syndrome in a Swedish School Population," *Developmental Medicine & Child Neurology* 45 (2003): 315–9; R. Kurlan, P. G. Como, B. Miller, D. Palumbo, C. Deeley, E. M. Andresen, et al., "The Behavioral Spectrum of Tic Disorders: a Community-based Study," *Neurology* 59 (2002): 414–20.

5. N. Khalifa and A. L. von Knorring, "Prevalence of Tic Disorders and Tourette Syndrome in a Swedish School Population," *Developmental Medicine & Child Neurology* 45 (2003): 315–9.

6. B. S. Peterson, H. Zhang, G. M. Anderson and J. F. Leckman, "A Double-blind, Placebo-controlled, Crossover Trial of an Antiandrogen in the Treatment of Tourette Syndrome," *Journal of Clinical Psychopharmacology* 18 (1998): 324–31; G. M. Alexander and B. S. Peterson, "Testing the Prenatal Hormone Hypothesis of Tic-related Disorders: Gender Identity and Gender Role Behavior," *Development and Psychopathology* 16 (2004): 407–20.

7. D. Staley, R. Wand, and G. Shady, "Tourette Disorder: A Cross-cultural Review," *Comprehensive Psychiatry* 38 (1997): 6–16.

8. R. Jin, R. Y. Zheng, W. W. Huang, H. Q. Xu, B. Shao, H. Chen, et al., "Epidemiological Survey of Tourette Syndrome in Children and Adolescents in Wenzhou of P. R. China," *European Journal of Epidemiology* 20 (2005): 925–7.

9. M. M. Robertson, "The Prevalence and Epidemiology of Gilles de la Tourette Syndrome. Part 1: The Epidemiological and Prevalence Studies," *Journal of Psychosomatic Research* 65 (2008): 461–72.

10. M. M. Robertson, "The Prevalence and Epidemiology of Gilles de la Tourette Syndrome. Part 2: Tentative Explanations for Differing Prevalence Figures in GTS, including the Possible Effects of Psychopathology, Aetiology, Cultural Differences, and Differing

Phenotypes," *Journal of Psychosomatic Research* 65 (2008): 473–86.

11. P. J. Hoekstra, M. P. Steenhuis, C. G. Kallenberg and R. B. Minderaa, "Association of Small Life Events with Self Reports of Tic Severity in Pediatric and Adult Tic Disorder Patients: A Prospective Longitudinal Study," *Journal of Clinical Psychiatry* 65 (2004): 426–31; H. Lin, L. Katsovich, M. Ghebremichael, D. B. Findley, H. Grantz, P. J. Lombroso, et al., "Psychosocial Stress Predicts Future Symptom Severities in Children and Adolescents with Tourette Syndrome and/or Obsessive-Compulsive Disorder," *Journal of Child Psychology & Psychiatry* 48 (2007): 157–66.

Chapter 4

1. L. Turtle and M. M. Robertson, "Tics, Twitches, Tales: The Experiences of Gilles de la Tourette Syndrome," *American Journal of Orthopsychiatry* 78 (2008): 449–55.

2. D. Keen-Kim and N. B. Freimer, "Genetics and Epidemiology of Tourette Syndrome," *Journal of Child Neurology* 21 (2006): 665–71.

3. R. A. Price, K. K. Kidd, D. J. Cohen, D. L. Pauls and J. F. Leckman, "A Twin Study of Tourette Syndrome," *Archives of General Psychiatry* 42 (1985): 815–20.

4. D. Keen-Kim and N. B. Freimer, "Genetics and Epidemiology of Tourette Syndrome," *Journal of Child Neurology* 21 (2006): 665–71.

5. H. S. Singer and K. Minzer, "Neurobiology of Tourette Syndrome: Concepts of Neuroanatomic Localization and Neurochemical Abnormalities," *Brain & Development* 25 Suppl 1 (2003): S70–84.

6. K. R. Muller-Vahl, G. J. Meyer, W. H. Knapp, H. M. Emrich, P. Gielow, T. Brucke, et al., "Serotonin Transporter Binding in Tourette Syndrome," *Neuroscience Letters* 385 (2005): 120–5.

7. P. Toren, A. Weizman, S. Ratner, D. Cohen, and N. Laor, "Ondansetron Treatment in Tourette Disorder: a 3-week, Randomized, Double-blind, Placebo-controlled Study," *Journal of Clinical Psychiatry* 66 (2005): 499–503.

8. A. R. Braun, C. Randolph, B. Stoetter, E. Mohr, C. Cox, K. Vladar, et al., "The Functional Neuroanatomy of Tourette Syndrome: An FDG-PET Study. II: Relationships between Regional Cerebral Metabolism and Associated Behavioral and Cognitive Features of the Illness," *Neuropsychopharmacology* 13 (1995): 151–68; A. R. Braun, B. Stoetter, C. Randolph, J. K. Hsiao, K. Vladar, J. Gernert, et al., "The Functional Neuroanatomy of Tourette Syndrome: An FDG-PET Study. I. Regional Changes in Cerebral Glucose Metabolism Differentiating Patients and Controls," *Neuropsychopharmacology* 9 (1993): 277–91; D. Eidelberg, J. R. Moeller, A. Antonini, K. Kazumata, V. Dhawan, C. Budman, et al., "The Metabolic Anatomy of Tourette Syndrome," *Neurology* 48 (1997): 927–34.

9. B. S. Peterson, P. Skudlarski, A. W. Anderson, H. Zhang, J.C. Gatenby,

C.M. Lacadie, et al., "A Functional Magnetic Resonance Imaging Study of Tic Suppression in Tourette Syndrome," *Archives of General Psychiatry* 55 (1998): 326–33; B. Biswal, J. L. Ulmer, R. L. Krippendorf, H. H. Harsch, D. L. Daniels, J. S. Hyde, et al., "Abnormal Cerebral Activation Associated with a Motor Task in Tourette Syndrome," *American Journal of Neuroradiology* 19 (1998): 1509–12.

10. K. A. Frey and R. L. Albin, "Neuroimaging of Tourette Syndrome," *Journal of Child Neurology* 21 (2006): 672–7; H. S. Singer, A. L. Reiss, J. E. Brown, E. H. Aylward, B. Shih, E. Chee, et al., "Volumetric MRI Changes in Basal Ganglia of Children with Tourette Syndrome," *Neurology* 43 (1993): 950–6; B. Peterson, M. A. Riddle, D. J. Cohen, L. D. Katz, J. C. Smith, M. T. Hardin, et al., "Reduced Basal Ganglia Volumes in Tourette's Syndrome using Three-dimensional Reconstruction Techniques from Magnetic Resonance Images," *Neurology* 43 (1993): 941–9; T. M. Hyde, M. E. Stacey, R. Coppola, S. F. Handel, K. C. Rickler, and D. R. Weinberger, "Cerebral Morphometric Abnormalities in Tourette's Syndrome: A Quantitative MRI Study of Monozygotic Twins," *Neurology* 45 (1995): 1176–82.

11. S. E. Swedo, H. L. Leonard, M. Garvey, B. Mittleman, A. J. Allen, S. Perlmutter, et al., "Pediatric Autoimmune Neuropsychiatric Disorders Associated with Streptococcal Infections: Clinical Description of the First 50 Cases," *American Journal of Psychiatry* 155 (1998): 264–71.

12. L. K. Mell, R. L. Davis and D. Owens, "Association Between Streptococcal Infection and Obsessive-Compulsive Disorder, Tourette's Syndrome, and Tic Disorder," *Pediatrics* 116 (2005): 56–60.

13. K. Harris and H. S. Singer, "Tic Disorders: Neural Circuits, Neurochemistry, and Neuroimmunology," *Journal of Child Neurology* 21 (2006): 678–89; J. E. Swain, L. Scahill, P. J. Lombroso, R. A. King and J. F. Leckman, "Tourette Syndrome and Tic Disorders: A Decade of Progress," *Journal of the American Academy of Child and Adolescent Psychiatry* 46 (2007): 947–68.

Chapter 5

1. J. E. Swain, L. Scahill, P. J. Lombroso, R. A. King and J.F . Leckman, "Tourette Syndrome and Tic Disorders: A Decade of Progress," *Journal of the American Academy of Child & Adolescent Psychiatry* 46 (2007): 947–68; P. Sandor, "Pharmacological Management of Tics in Patients with TS," *Journal of Psychosomatic Research* 55 (2003): 41–8; M. H. Bloch, "Emerging Treatments for Tourette's Disorder," *Current Psychiatry Reports* 10 (2008): 323–30; D. Gilbert, "Treatment of Children and Adolescents with Tics and Tourette Syndrome," *Journal of Child Neurology* 21 (2006): 690–700.

2. J. E. Swain, L. Scahill, P. J. Lombroso, R. A. King and J. F. Leckman,

"Tourette Syndrome and Tic Disorders: A Decade of Progress," *Journal of the American Academy of Child & Adolescent Psychiatry* 46 (2007): 947–68; P. Sandor, "Pharmacological Management of Tics in Patients with TS," *Journal of Psychosomatic Research* 55 (2003): 41–8.

3. J. E. Swain, L. Scahill, P. J. Lombroso, R. A. King and J. F. Leckman, "Tourette Syndrome and Tic Disorders: A Decade of Progress," *Journal of the American Academy of Child & Adolescent Psychiatry* 46 (2007): 947–68; P. Sandor, "Pharmacological Management of Tics in Patients with TS," *Journal of Psychosomatic Research* 55 (2003): 41–8; M. H. Bloch, "Emerging Treatments for Tourette's Disorder," *Current Psychiatry Reports* 10 (2008): 323–30; D. Gilbert, "Treatment of Children and Adolescents with Tics and Tourette Syndrome," *Journal of Child Neurology* 21 (2006): 690–700.

4. P. R. Sanberg, A. A. Silver, R. D. Shytle, M. K. Philipp, D. W. Cahill, H. M. Fogelson, et al., "Nicotine for the Treatment of Tourette's Syndrome," *Pharmacology & Therapeutics* 74 (1997): 21–5.

5. A. A. Silver and P. R. Sanberg, "Transdermal Nicotine Patch and Potentiation of Haloperidol in Tourette's Syndrome," *Lancet* 342 (1993): 182.

6. R. Sandyk and G. Awerbuch, "Marijuana and Tourette's Syndrome," *Journal of Clinical Psychopharmacology* 8 (1988): 444–5.

7. K. R. Muller-Vahl, U. Schneider, A. Koblenz, M. Jobges, H. Kolbe, T. Daldrup, et al., "Treatment of Tourette's Syndrome with Delta 9-tetrahydrocannabinol (THC): A Randomized Crossover Trial," *Pharmacopsychiatry* 35 (2002): 57–61.

8. S. J. Perlmutter, S. F. Leitman, M. A. Garvey, S. Hamburger, E. Feldman, H. L. Leonard, et al., "Therapeutic Plasma Exchange and Intravenous Immunoglobulin for Obsessive-Compulsive Disorder and Tic Disorders in Childhood," *Lancet* 354 (1999): 1153–8; N. Muller, M. Riedel, A. Erfurth and H. J. Moller, "Immunoglobulin Therapy in Gilles de la Tourette Syndrome," *Nervenarzt* 68 (1997): 914–6.

9. N. Muller, "Anti-inflammatory Therapy with a COX-2 Inhibitor in Tourette's Syndrome," *Inflammopharmacology* 12 (2004): 271–5.

10. M. L. Murphy and M. E. Pichichero, "Prospective Identification and Treatment of Children with Pediatric Autoimmune Neuropsychiatric Disorder Associated with Group A Streptococcal Infection (PANDAS)," *Archives of Pediatrics & Adolescent Medicine* 156 (2002): 356–61; N. Muller, M. Riedel, S. Forderreuther, C. Blendinger and M. Abele-Horn, "Tourette's Syndrome and Mycoplasma Pneumoniae Infection," *American Journal of Psychiatry* 157 (2000): 481–2.

11. M. Rapoport, V. Feder, and P. Sandor, "Response of Major Depression and Tourette's Syndrome to ECT: A Case Report,"

Psychosomatic Medicine 60 (1998): 528–9; H. K. Trivedi, A. J. Mendelowitz and M. Fink, "Gilles de la Tourette Form of Catatonia: Response to ECT," *Journal of ECT* 19 (2003): 115–7; M. Strassnig, M. Riedel, and N. Muller N, "Electroconvulsive Therapy in a Patient with Tourette's Syndrome and Co-morbid Obsessive Compulsive Disorder," *World Journal of Biological Psychiatry* 5 (2004): 164–6.

12. N. R. Swerdlow and A. N. Sutherland, "Using Animal Models to Develop Therapeutics for Tourette Syndrome," *Pharmacology & Therapeutics* 108 (2005): 281–93; N. R. Swerdlow and A. N. Sutherland, "Preclinical Models Relevant to Tourette Syndrome," *Advanced Neurology* 99 (2006): 69–88.

13. J. R. Taylor, S. A. Morshed, S. Parveen, M. T. Mercadante, L. Scahill, B. S. Peterson, et al., "An Animal Model of Tourette's Syndrome," *American Journal of Psychiatry* 159 (2002): 657–60.

14. K. C. Berridge, J. W. Aldridge, K. R. Houchard, and X. Zhuang, "Sequential Super-stereotypy of an Instinctive Fixed Action Pattern in Hyper-dopaminergic Mutant Mice: A Model of Obsessive Compulsive Disorder and Tourette's," *BMC Biology* 3 (2005): 4.

15. L. Ackermans, Y. Temel, and V. Visser-Vandewalle, "Deep Brain Stimulation in Tourette's Syndrome," *Neurotherapeutics* 5 (2008): 339–44; J. S. Neimat, P. G. Patil, and A. M. Lozano, "Novel Surgical Therapies for Tourette Syndrome,"

Journal of Child Neurology 21 (2006): 715–8.

16. A. Mantovani, S. H. Lisanby, F. Pieraccini, M. Ulivelli, P. Castrogiovanni, and S. Rossi, "Repetitive Transcranial Magnetic Stimulation (rTMS) in the Treatment of Obsessive-Compulsive Disorder (OCD) and Tourette's Syndrome (TS)," *International Journal of Neuropsychopharmacol* 9 (2006): 95–100; J. H. Chae, Z. Nahas, E. Wassermann, X. Li, G. Sethuraman, D. Gilbert, et al., "A Pilot Safety Study of Repetitive Transcranial Magnetic Stimulation (rTMS) in Tourette's Syndrome," *Cognitive & Behavioral Neurology* 17 (2004): 109–17.

17. S. Anandan, C. L. Wigg, C. R. Thomas, and B. Coffey, "Psychosurgery for Self-injurious Behavior in Tourette's Disorder," *Journal of Child & Adolescent Psychopharmacology* 14 (2004): 531–8; Y. Temel and V. Visser-Vandewalle, "Surgery in Tourette Syndrome," *Movement Disorders* 19 (2004): 3–14.

18. Y. Temel and V. Visser-Vandewalle, "Surgery in Tourette Syndrome," *Movement Disorders* 19 (2004): 3–14.

Chapter 6

1. J. Piacentini and S. Chang, "Behavioral Treatments for Tourette Syndrome and Tic Disorders: State of the Art," *Advanced Neurology* 85 (2001): 319–31.

2. Ibid.

3. C. A. Conelea and D. W. Woods, "The Influence of Contextual Factors on Tic Expression in Tourette's Syndrome: A Review," *Journal of*

Psychosomatic Research 65 (2008): 487–96.

4. A. L. Peterson and N. H. Azrin, "An Evaluation of Behavioral Treatments for Tourette Syndrome," *Behaviour Research & Therapy* 30 (1992): 167–74.

5. R. E. Davis and I. Osorio, "Childhood Caffeine Tic Syndrome," *Pediatrics* 101 (1998): E4.

6. G.S. Golden, "The Effect of Central Nervous System Stimulants on Tourette Syndrome," *Annals of Neurology* 2 (1977): 69–70; T. L. Lowe, D. J. Cohen, J. Detlor, M. W. Kremenitzer, and B. A. Shaywitz, "Stimulant Medications Precipitate Tourette's Syndrome," *Journal of the American Medical Assocciation* 247 (1982): 1729–31; F. E. Cardoso and J. Jankovic, "Cocaine-related Movement Disorders," *Movement Disorders* 8 (1993): 175–8.

7. J. Piacentini and S. Chang, "Behavioral Treatments for Tourette Syndrome and Tic Disorders: State of the Art," *Advanced Neurology* 85 (2001): 319–31; J. Piacentini and S. Chang, "Habit Reversal Training for Tic Disorders in Children and Adolescents," *Behavior Modification* 29 (2005): 803–22; J. C. Piacentini and S. W. Chang, "Behavioral Treatments for Tic Suppression: Habit Reversal Training," *Advanced Neurology* 99 (2006): 227–33; M. B. Himle, D. W. Woods, J. C. Piacentini, and J. T. Walkup, "Brief Review of Habit Reversal Training for Tourette Syndrome," *Journal of Child Neurology* 21 (2006): 719–25.

8. N. H. Azrin and R. G. Nunn, "Habit-Reversal: A Method of Eliminating Nervous Habits and Tics," *Behaviour Research & Therapy* 11 (1973): 619–28.

9. M. B. Himle, D. W. Woods, J. C. Piacentini, and J. T. Walkup, "Brief Review of Habit Reversal Training for Tourette Syndrome," *Journal of Child Neurology* 21 (2006): 719–25.

Chapter 7

1. C. Gaze, H. O. Kepley, and J. T. Walkup, "Co-occurring Psychiatric Disorders in Children and Adolescents with Tourette Syndrome," *Journal of Child Neurology* 21 (2006): 657–64.

2. M. M. Robertson, "Mood Disorders and Gilles de la Tourette's Syndrome: An Update on Prevalence, Etiology, Comorbidity, Clinical Associations, and Implications," *Journal of Psychosomatic Research* 61 (2006): 349–58.

3. C. Gaze, H. O. Kepley, and J. T. Walkup, "Co-occurring Psychiatric Disorders in Children and Adolescents with Tourette Syndrome," *Journal of Child Neurology* 21 (2006): 657–64.

4. B. Kadesjo and C. Gillberg, "Tourette's Disorder: Epidemiology and Comorbidity in Primary School Children," *Journal of the American Academy of Child & Adolescent Psychiatry* 39 (2000): 548–55; D. M. Sheppard, J. L. Bradshaw, R. Purcell and C. Pantelis, "Tourette's and Comorbid Syndromes: Obsessive Compulsive and Attention Deficit Hyperactivity Disorder.

A Common Etiology?" *Clinical Psychology Review* 19 (1999): 531–52.

5. M. B. Denckla, "Attention-deficit Hyperactivity Disorder (ADHD) Comorbidity: A Case for "Pure" Tourette Syndrome?" *Journal of Child Neurology* 21 (2006): 701–3.

6. Ibid.

7. W. R. Kates, I. S. Warsofsky, A. Patwardhan, M. T. Abrams, A. M. Liu, S. Naidu, et al., "Automated Talairach Atlas-based Parcellation and Measurement of Cerebral Lobes in Children," *Psychiatry Research* 91 (1999): 11–30.

8. M. B. Denckla, "Attention-deficit Hyperactivity Disorder (ADHD) Comorbidity: A Case for 'Pure' Tourette Syndrome?" *Journal of Child Neurology* 21 (2006): 701–3.

9. Group TSS, "Treatment of ADHD in Children with Tics: A Randomized Controlled Trial," *Neurology* 58 (2002): 527–36.

10. N. D. Volkow, G. J. Wang, J. S. Fowler, and Y. S. Ding, "Imaging the Effects of Methylphenidate on Brain Dopamine: New Model on its Therapeutic Actions for Attention-deficit/Hyperactivity Disorder," *Biological Psychiatry* 57 (2005): 1410–5.

11. S. H. Kollins, "Abuse Liability of Medications Used to Treat Attention-deficit/Hyperactivity Disorder (ADHD)," *American Journal on Addictions* 16 Suppl 1 (2007): 35–42; quiz 43–4.

12. W. K. Goodman, E. A. Storch, G. R. Geffken, and T.K. Murphy, "Obsessive-compulsive Disorder in Tourette Syndrome," *Journal of Child Neurology* 21 (2006): 704–14.

13. J. F. Leckman, D. E. Grice, L. C. Barr, A. L. de Vries, C. Martin, D. J. Cohen, et al., "Tic-related vs. Non-tic-related Obsessive Compulsive Disorder," *Anxiety* 1 (1994): 208–15; E. C. Miguel, L. Baer, B. J. Coffey, S. L. Rauch, C. R. Savage, R. L. O'Sullivan, et al., "Phenomenological Differences Appearing with Repetitive Behaviours in Obsessive-compulsive Disorder and Gilles de la Tourette's Syndrome," *British Journal of Psychiatry* 170 (1997): 140–5.

14. E. C. Miguel, M. C. do Rosario-Campos, H. S. Prado, R. do Valle, S. L. Rauch, B. J. Coffey, et al., "Sensory Phenomena in Obsessive-compulsive Disorder and Tourette's Disorder," *Journal of Clinical Psychiatry* 61 (2000): 150–6; quiz 157.

15. W. K. Goodman, E. A. Storch, G. R. Geffken, and T. K. Murphy, "Obsessive-compulsive Disorder in Tourette Syndrome," *Journal of Child Neurology* 21 (2006): 704–14.

16. M. M. Robertson, "Mood Disorders and Gilles de la Tourette's Syndrome: An Update on Prevalence, Etiology, Comorbidity, Clinical Associations, and Implications," *Journal of Psychosomatic Research* 61 (2006): 349–58; D. L. Wodrich, E. Benjamin, and D. Lachar, "Tourette's Syndrome and Psychopathology in a Child Psychiatry Setting," *Journal of the American Academy of Child & Adolescent Psychiatry* 36 (1997): 1618–24.

17. B. J. Coffey, J. Biederman, J. W. Smoller, D. A. Geller, P. Sarin, S. Schwartz, et al., "Anxiety Disorders and Tic severity in Juveniles with

Tourette's Disorder," *Journal of the American Academy of Child & Adolescent Psychiatry* 39 (2000): 562–8.

18. J. F. Leckman, M. H. Bloch, L. Scahill, and R. A. King, "Tourette Syndrome: The Self Under Siege," *Journal of Child Neurology* 21 (2006): 642–9.

19. R. D. Freeman, D. K. Fast, L. Burd, J. Kerbeshian, M. M. Robertson, and P. Sandor, "An International Perspective on Tourette Syndrome: Selected Findings from 3,500 Individuals in 22 Countries," *Developmental Medicine and Child Neurology* 42 (2000): 436–47; P. Szatmari, D. R. Offord, and M. H. Boyle, "Ontario Child Health Study: Prevalence of Attention Deficit Disorder with Hyperactivity," *Journal of Child Psychology & Psychiatry* 30 (1989): 219–30.

20. J. Jankovic, C. Kwak, and R. R. Frankoff, "Tourette's Syndrome and the Law," *Journal of Neuropsychiatry and Clinical Neurosciences* 18 (2006): 86–95.

21. L. Scahill, D. G. Sukhodolsky, K. Bearss, D. Findley, V. Hamrin, D. H. Carroll, et al., "Randomized Trial of Parent Management Training in Children with Tic Disorders and Disruptive Behavior," *Journal of Child Neurology* 21 (2006): 650–6.

22. S. Cohrs, T. Rasch, S. Altmeyer, J. Kinkelbur, T. Kostanecka, A. Rothenberger, et al., "Decreased Sleep Quality and Increased Sleep Related Movements in Patients with Tourette's Syndrome," *Journal of Neurology, Neurosurgery & Psychiatry* 70 (2001): 192–7; T. Kostanecka-Endress, T. Banaschewski, J. Kinkelbur, I. Wullner, S. Lichtblau, S. Cohrs, et al., "Disturbed Sleep in Children with Tourette Syndrome: a Polysomnographic Study," *Journal of Psychosomatic Research* 55 (2003): 23–9; A. Rothenberger, T. Kostanecka, J. Kinkelbur, S. Cohrs, W. Woerner, and G. Hajak, "Sleep and Tourette Syndrome," *Advanced Neurology* 85 (2001): 245–59.

Chapter 8

1. U. Chowdhury. *Tics and Tourette Syndrome —A Handbook for Parents and Professionals* (Philadelphia: Jessica Kingsley Publishers, 2004).

2. Ibid.

GLOSSARY

Adderall—Stimulant medication consisting of a mixture of various forms of amphetamines; used to treat ADHD.

akathisia—Feelings of inner restlessness.

antibodies—Proteins that are made by cells in the immune system that recognize specific molecules, such as those on the surface of bacteria cells, that target those cells' destruction by other cells of the immune system.

antipsychotic—Medication that reduces the symptoms of psychosis, such as paranoia, delusions, and hallucinations; also called a neuroleptic.

attention-deficit/ hyperactivity disorder (ADHD)—A psychiatric disorder characterized by hyperactivity, impulsivity, an inability to focus one's attention or concentrate, easily being distracted, and often showing disruptive behaviors; ADHD is commonly associated with TS.

autoimmune disorder—A medical condition in which the immune system mistakenly attacks the body's natural healthy tissues and organs.

awareness training—Behavioral therapy technique used to teach TS patients to become aware of when he or she executes a tic.

axon—Long, wire-like fiber extension of a neuron that conducts electrical signals.

basal ganglia—A collection of structures deep within the brain that control voluntary movements.

bullying—Repeated intentional insulting, threatening, name-calling, humiliating, or even physically harming of an individual by another person.

chromosome—The structures in living cells that contain DNA.

chronic motor tic disorder (CMTD)—Similar to TS but symptoms only include motor tics.

chronic vocal tic disorder (CVTD)—Similar to TS but symptoms only include vocal tics.

cingulotomy—Surgical removal of part of the brain called the cingulum.

cingulum—Part of the brain that when removed (called a cingulotomy), reduces the severity of tics.

comorbidity—The occurrence of more than one medical condition in the same patient.

competing response—Behavioral therapy technique in which patients, upon feeling a premonitory urge, purposely move the affected body part (arm, leg, etc.) in the direction opposite to that which the tic normally causes involuntary movement.

compulsion—A behavior that is performed repeatedly in an attempt to neutralize the anxiety provoked by an obsession, such as repeatedly washing one's hands after having obsessions about being contaminated with germs; one of the primary symptoms of obsessive-compulsive disorder.

contingency management—Type of behavioral therapy for TS where extended periods of time in which tics do not occur are rewarded; sometimes called operant conditioning.

coprolalia—Repeated blurting out of obscenities or curse words; a type of vocal tic.

deep brain stimulation (DBS)—A neurosurgical technique that uses an electrode implanted into the brain to overstimulate nerve cells, which causes them to shut down and become inactivated.

deep breathing exercises—Behavioral technique used to reduce stress and anxiety.

dizygotic twin—A person whose fetus developed following the fertilization of two separate eggs.

dopamine—A chemical messenger in the brain that is known to be involved in TS.

dysphoria—Strong unpleasant mood or feelings.

dystonia—Prolonged, painful muscle contractions.

echolalia—Imitating or repeating sounds or words spoken by another individual; can occur repeatedly as a type of vocal tic.

electroconvulsive therapy (ECT)—A technique used by psychiatrists and neurologists to pass large amounts of electrical current through the brain to reduce the symptoms of brain disorders such as depression or TS.

epidemiology—The study of the frequency and severity of a disorder, disease, or other health problem across cultures, ethnicities, ages, genders, socioeconomic status, and geography.

exposure plus response prevention—Behavioral therapy technique for treating OCD that consists of intentionally exposing the patient to something he or she is frightened of and then disallowing any type of compulsive response that the patient uses to relieve the provoked anxiety.

frontal cortex—Foremost part of the brain that is involved in thinking, planning, impulse control, decision making, and certain types of memory.

gamma globulin—A protein that, when given in high doses, overloads the immune system so that it cannot attack the body's own tissue and organs, as is the case in autoimmune disorders.

gene—A sequence of DNA that codes, or forms the blueprint for, the production of a specific protein.

guided imagery—Behavioral and psychological technique used to reduce stress and anxiety.

habit reversal therapy—Behavioral therapy technique used to voluntarily control tics.

leucotomy—*See* **lobotomy**.

lobotomy—Surgical removal of the frontal cortex; also called leucotomy.

magnetic resonance imaging (MRI)—A technique for imaging the brain that detects increased blood flow to regions of the brain that are more active than nonactive regions.

malignant Tourette syndrome—A form of TS in which the tic involves physical harming of the self or others.

massed practice—A behavioral therapy used to treat TS by having the patient purposely and repeatedly perform a tic so as to cause fatigue in the muscle groups involved in executing the tic, thereby providing temporary relief.

methylphenidate—Mild stimulant, sold in the United States under the brand name of Ritalin.

monozygotic twin—A person whose fetus developed by the splitting of a fertilized egg into two separate developing embryos.

morphometry—A brain imaging technique that allows for the determination of the size of individual brain structures; also known as volumetric MRI.

motor tic—Repetitive, meaningless movements of parts of the body; can be simple, such as nose-twitching, eye blinking, and jerking of the head or arms, or complex, such as spinning 360 degrees in a circle or doing deep knee bends.

neuroleptic—Medication that reduces the symptoms of psychosis, such as paranoia, delusions, and hallucinations; also called an antipsychotic.

neuron—Nerve cell.

neurotransmitter—A chemical messenger that carries a signal from one neuron to another.

obsession—A repeated, intrusive, unwanted thought or fear of harming someone, being contaminated by germs, vulgar sexual acts, or blasphemy; one of the primary symptoms of obsessive-compulsive disorder.

obsessive-compulsive disorder (OCD)—A psychiatric disorder characterized by repeated, unwanted, intrusive thoughts (obsessions) that provoke anxiety and often compel the person to repeatedly perform an act (a compulsion) in an attempt to neutralize the thought and resulting anxiety; OCD commonly co-occurs with TS.

operant conditioning—Type of behavioral therapy for TS where extended periods of time in which tics do not occur are rewarded; sometimes called contingency management.

oppositional defiant disorder—A behavioral disorder in children characterized by refusing to obey one's parents, impulsivity, explosive outbursts, tantrums, and sudden attacks of physical and emotional rage against parents or other figures of authority.

palilalia—Repetition of words or sentence spoken by oneself; can occur repeatedly as a type of vocal tic.

pediatric autoimmune neuropsychiatric disorder associated with streptococcal infection (PANDAS)—An autoimmune disorder that is still debated regarding whether or not it can cause TS in some individuals.

phonic tic—See **vocal tic**.

positron emission tomography (PET)—A method for imaging the brain or other body parts by detecting the use of a radioactively labeled substance such as sugar or water by cells.

post-traumatic stress disorder (PTSD)—Psychological disorder resulting from experiencing or witnessing a traumatic even; characterized by flashbacks of the traumatic event, avoidance of locations, places, or people associated with the event, and heightened levels of anxiety.

premonitory urge—An uncomfortable sensory feeling in the part of the body where a tic occurs that builds in intensity, and is relieved by performing the tic.

progressive muscle relaxation—Behavioral technique used to reduce stress and anxiety.

pseudoephedrine—A mild stimulant commonly used in nasal decongestants.

psychosurgery—Surgery on the brain in which parts of the brain that are suspected to be functioning abnormally are destroyed or removed.

receptor—A specialized protein that recognizes and binds to a specific neurotransmitter and causes the neuron on which it is located to become activated or inactivated.

relaxation training—Behavioral technique used to reduce stress and anxiety; usually consists of deep breathing exercises, progressive muscle relaxation, or guided imagery.

repetitive transcranial magnetic stimulation (rTMS)—A technique that uses pulses of magnetic waves to repeatedly stimulate specific areas of the outer portion of the brain.

Ritalin—Brand name (U.S.) for methylphenidate.

selective serotonin reuptake inhibitors (SSRIs)—Medications used to treat depression and OCD that block the ability of neurons to reabsorb the neurotransmitter serotonin after it has been released at a synapse.

self-injurious behavior (SIB)—Intentional or unintentional harming of the self, such as cutting one's skin with a knife or banging one's head against a wall; is characteristic of malignant Tourette syndrome.

serotonin—A chemical messenger within the brain possibly involved in TS.

Streptococcus pyogenes—A type of bacteria that causes strep throat and which may in some children cause the immune system to attack the body's own cells.

synapse—A junction or connection between nerve cells that uses special chemical messengers called neurotransmitters.

synaptic terminal—A mushroom-shaped ending of an axon that releases neurotransmitters.

tardive dyskinesia—Repetitive, purposeless movements that resembles tics in TS patients, but are caused by a side effect of a neuroleptic.

thalamotomy—Surgical removal of a region of the brain called the thalamus.

thalamus—Part of the brain that, when removed (called a thalamotomy), reduces the severity of tics.

tic—An involuntary, repeated, senseless movement of the head, neck, arms, legs, hands, or face, or even an orchestrated sequence of movements (all of these are called motor tics), or involuntary, repeated vocalizations such as grunting, using obscenities, or uttering nonsense phrases (these are called vocal or phonic tics).

tic hierarchy—A prioritized list of a TS patient's tics ranked in order by the amount of distress each one causes.

Tourette syndrome (TS)—A neurological disorder with onset of symptoms during childhood or adolescence, primarily characterized by vocal and motor tics.

transcranial magnetic stimulation (TMS)—A technique that uses pulses of magnetic waves to stimulate specific areas of the outer portion of the brain; can be done repeatedly, in which case it is referred to as repetitive TMS (rTMS).

transient tic disorder (TTD)—Disorder similar to TS but characterized by tics that last at least four weeks but less than 12 months.

transporter—A protein located on a synaptic terminal that reabsorbs neurotransmitters after their release so as to terminate the neurotransmitter signal and reuse it for future nerve impulses.

vocal tic—A repetitive, meaningless utterance of a sound, word or phrase; can be simple, such as grunt or a chirp, or complex, such as phrase of several words; sometimes referred to as a phonic tic.

volumetric MRI—A brain imaging technique that allows for the determination of the size of individual brain structures; also known as morphometry.

zygote—A fertilized egg that will develop into a fetus.

Books

Brill, M. T. *Tourette Syndrome.* Brookfield, Conn.: Twenty-First Century Books, 2002.

Chowdhury, U. *Tics and Tourette Syndrome—A Handbook for Parents and Professionals.* Philadelphia: Jessica Kingsley Publishers, 2004.

Handler, L. *Twitch and Shout—A Touretter's Tale.* New York: Dutton Publishers, 1998.

Kushner, H.I. *A Cursing Brain? The Histories of Tourette Syndrome.* Cambridge, Mass.: Harvard University Press, 1999.

Landau, E. *Tourette Syndrome.* Danbury, Conn.: Franklin Watts, 1998.

Moe, B. *Coping with Tourette Syndrome and Tic Disorders.* New York: Rosen Publishing Group, 2000.

Web Sites

National Institute of Mental Health: Attention-Deficit/Hyperactivity Disorder
http://www.nimh.nih.gov/health/topics/attention-deficit-hyperactivity-disorder-adhd/index.shtml

National Institute of Mental Health: Obsessive-Compulsive Disorder
http://www.nimh.nih.gov/health/topics/obsessive-compulsive-disorder-ocd/index.shtml

National Institute on Neurological Disease and Stroke: Tourette Syndrome Fact Sheet
http://www.ninds.nih.gov/disorders/tourette/detail_tourette.htm

National Tourette Syndrome Association (United States)
http://www.tsa-usa.org

Neuroscience for Kids—Tourette Syndrome
http://faculty.washington.edu/chudler/ts.html

Tourette Syndrome "Plus"
http://www.tourettesyndrome.net

INDEX

concentration, lack of, 75

contingency management. *See* operant conditioning

coprolalia, 14

counseling and TS, 76, 77, 84

CR. *See* competing response

CVTD. *See* chronic vocal tic disorder

Dampierre, Marquise de, 4, 14

Davis, Richard, 56

DBS. *See* deep brain stimulation

deep brain stimulation (DBS), 44–47, 49

deep breathing exercises, 54–55

delta-9-tetrahydrocannabinol. *See* THC

dementia, ix

depression

   brain connections, vi

   bullying, 82

   deep brain stimulation, 46

   electroconvulsive therapy, 43

   malignant Tourette syndrome, 13

   medication side effect, 39

   rTMS as treatment, 48

   TS and, 61, 67–68, 72

Diagnostic and Statistical Manual of Mental Disorders (DSM-IV), 10

disruptive behavior, 61, 69–70, 72, 80

dizygotic twins, 27

dizziness, 39

DNA, 26, 27

dopamine

   basal ganglia, 30

   brain abnormalities, 28, 35

   described, 6

   imbalance, 63

   receptors, 36–37, 49

DSM-IV. *See Diagnostic and Statistical Manual of Mental Disorders*

drug addiction, vi

dysphoria, 39

dystonia, 39

echolalia, 14

ECT. *See* electroconvulsive therapy

education

   of family members, 6, 37, 50, 74–76, 84

   friends/classmates, 6, 50, 75–76, 79–80

   teachers, 37, 50, 78–81, 84

   TS patient, 6, 50, 76, 84

electroconvulsive therapy (ECT), 43–44, 45, 47, 49

environment and brain development, vi

epidemiology of TS, 19

epilepsy, vi, 48. *See also* seizures

exercise techniques, 6

exposure plus response prevention, 65

facial expressions, 9, 11, 12

family and TS, 18, 36, 74–76

fears. *See* obsessions

fluphenazine, 38. *See also* neuroleptics

fraternal twins, 27

frontal cortex, 49

GABHS. *See* Group A beta-hemolytic streptococci

gamma globulin, 43

Gehrig's disease, Lou, 33

gender and TS, 20, 21–23

genes

   brain development, vi, vii, 8

   defined, 27

   factors, 25–27

   TS as neurological condition, 19, 22, 75, 78

Gilles de la Tourette syndrome, 5. *See also* Tourette syndrome

girls and TS, 20, 23

grimacing, 11, 12. *See also* facial expressions

Group A beta-hemolytic streptococci (GABHS), 34

grunting. *See* Tourette syndrome, symptoms

ABOUT THE AUTHOR

M. Foster Olive received his bachelor's degree in psychology from the University of California at San Diego, and went on to receive his Ph.D. in neuroscience from the University of California–Los Angeles. He is currently an assistant professor in the Center for Drug and Alcohol Programs and Department of Psychiatry and Behavioral Sciences at the Medical University of South Carolina. Dr. Olive's research focuses on the neurobiology of drug addiction, and he has published in numerous academic journals, including *Nature Neuroscience, Neuropsychopharmacology,* and the *Journal of Neuroscience.*